Advance Praise for Amy James's Knowledge Essentials Series

"Knowledge Essentials is a remarkable series that will benefit children of all abilities and learning styles. Amy James has taken a close look at curriculum standards and testing around the country and developed simple and creative activities that support what's being taught at each grade level, while remaining sensitive to the fact that children learn at different rates and in different ways. I highly recommend it for all parents who want to make a difference in their children's education."

—Michael Gurian, author of *Boys and Girls Learn Differently* and *The Wonder of Boys*

"Finally, a book about teaching young children by somebody who knows her stuff! I can (and will) wholeheartedly recommend this series to the ever-growing number of parents who ask me for advice about how they can help their children succeed in elementary school."

—LouAnne Johnson, author of *Dangerous Minds* and *The Queen of Education*

"Having examined state standards nationwide, Amy James has created innovative and unique games and exercises to help children absorb what they *have* to learn, in ways that will help them *want* to learn. Individualized to the child's own learning style, this is a must-have series for parents who want to maximize their child's ability to succeed in and out of the classroom."

—Myrna B. Shure, Ph.D., author of *Thinking Parents, Thinking Child*

"The books in Amy James's timely and unique Knowledge Essentials series give parents a clear idea of what their children are learning and provide the tools they need to help their children live up to their full academic potential. This is must reading for any parent with a school-age child."

—Michele Borba, Ed.D., author of *Nobody Likes Me, Everybody Hates Me* and *No More Misbehavin'*

KINDERGARTEN SUCCESS

Everything You Need to Know to Help Your Child Learn

AMY JAMES

JOSSEY-BASS
A Wiley Imprint
www.josseybass.com

Published by Jossey-Bass
A Wiley Imprint
989 Market Street, San Francisco, CA 94103-1741
www.josseybass.com

Jossey-Bass books and products are available through most bookstores. To contact Jossey-Bass directly call our Customer Care Department within the U.S. at 800-956-7739, outside the U.S. at 317-572-3986, or fax 317-572-4002.

Jossey-Bass also publishes its books in a variety of electronic formats. Some content that appears in print may not be available in electronic books.

Library of Congress Cataloging-in-Publication Data

James, Amy, 1967–
  Kindergarten success: everything you need to know to help your child learn / Amy James.
      p. cm.—(Knowledge essentials)
  Includes bibliographical references and index.
  ISBN-13: 978-0-471-74813-7 (pbk.)
  ISBN-10: 0-471-74813-7 (pbk.)
  1. Kindergarten—Curricula—United States. 2. Kindergarten—Parent participation.
I. Title. II. Series: James, Amy, 1967– Knowledge essentials.
  LB1180.J36 2006
  372.21'8—dc22

                                                                    2006010536

Printed in the United States of America
FIRST EDITION
PB Printing 10 9 8 7 6 5 4 3 2 1

To my stepfather, Jim (Sky) King

CONTENTS

ACKNOWLEDGMENTS

I would like to thank the following people for advising me on this book:

Cindy King is a retired early childhood and reading specialist who taught kindergarten and first grade for thirty years. She assisted in establishing the transition program at her school district, a program for children who are developmentally young.

E. W. James was an elementary school principal and elementary school teacher for fifteen years. He led the school district's efforts to serve children with special needs.

Elizabeth Hecox is in her sixteenth year of teaching at Kennedy Elementary School in Norman, Oklahoma. She is an incredible classroom teacher, and the book is better because of her work with me on it.

Kim Lindsay is in her twelfth year of teaching elementary school in Dallas Public Schools and in Norman Public Schools. She was elected Teacher of the Year at Kennedy Elementary School in the 2001–2002 school year.

Pam Davidson retired from Norman Public Schools after spending 15 years in the classroom and 10 years as an elementary school principal. Pam has been a valued family friend for over 30 years and I am grateful that she is here to help me with this book series.

The employees at Six Things, Inc., are a group of thirty current and former teachers who provide invaluable assistance on a daily basis. Anytime I needed help in any subject area, for any grade, their enormously good brains were at my disposal. This book series would not be possible without their assistance, and I am eternally grateful to them for their help.

Introduction

Time really does fly, right? You were just teaching your baby to walk, rejoicing at his or her first spoken words, and joining playgroups, and here you are the parent of a kindergartner. You are debating the benefits of full-day versus half-day sessions, deciding if you have time to be a homeroom parent, and buying school supplies. How did your child grow up so fast?

Now your baby is starting school—real school—with buses, big kids, and bathroom passes. How will you both survive? Is there a place for you in your child's education? Is a teaching certificate a prerequisite for helping with homework? Where is the closest boarding school?

Relax, calm down, and stay in control. I think we all realize that your home is probably the single most important learning environment your child will be in and that parents are the single most important teachers. You and the learning environment you create in your home need to accommodate your child's growth and increasing skill levels.

As a parent, you are a primary caregiver, role model, and provider. Your kindergartner looks to you as the final authority; the last word; the smartest, strongest, prettiest, or most handsome person he or she knows. Learning environments are important. Whether your child is at school, at home, or in the car, the way you interact with your little learner will influence his or her abilities for a lifetime.

To effectively enhance your child's learning, you need to be constantly and consistently aware of your child's development over the years so that you can come to know his or her particular strengths, shortcomings, and areas of talent and natural inclination. And just because you know one of your children does not mean you know them all. Children's minds differ substantially from their siblings'. Each child is his or her own person with a unique set of abilities. As you gain insights into your children's development, you can easily help each child strengthen abilities while closing any important gaps or concentrating on areas of difficulty.

Life at home matters. An academically progressive home life is the key to effectively tracking your child's development as well as providing opportunities to successfully apply knowledge. Creating the environment is not about tutoring but about creating opportunities to learn and apply learning. The point is to bring the level of content and conversation in your daily life to the level that is in your child's school life. Home, your child's first learning environment, is the primary testing ground for new knowledge and skill sets.

Getting the Most from This Book

This book is a guide to creating an exceptional learning environment in your home. It contains curricula and skills unique to kindergarten presented in a way that makes it easy to put what you learn into practice immediately. This book serves as a tool to help solve the mystery behind creating a supportive, learning-rich environment in your home that fosters a thinking child's development while enriching his or her curricula. It contains dozens of mini–lesson plans that include easy-to-use activities designed to help your child meet your state's learning requirements. An environmental learning section in each chapter tells you how to identify learning opportunities in the everyday world.

Chapters 2 through 4 of the book give you some child development information to get you started. Teaching is about knowing the subject area you teach, but moreover it is about knowing the abilities of the students you teach. As a parent you can easily see the milestones your child reaches at an early age (crawling, walking, talking, and so on), but milestones are not always apparent in your five- and six-year-old. These chapters explain the child development processes that take place during kindergarten, including what thinking milestones your child's brain is capable of and will reach in normal development during this time. In order for you to teach effectively, you will need to account for these developmental milestones in all topics and skills that you introduce.

Teaching is also about recognizing how different people learn and tailoring the way you teach to suit them. You will find out how to recognize different learning styles in chapter 3, which will help you implement the learning activities in the rest of the book.

Chapters 5 through 9 provide general subject area information for the kindergarten curriculum. The curriculum discussed in this book was chosen by reviewing all fifty of the state learning standards, the National Subject Area Association learning standards, the core curriculum materials that many school districts use, and supplemental education products. Although there are some discrepancies in curricula from region to region, they are few and far between. Chances are that even if you aren't able to use all the topical subject area units (such as social studies and science), you will be able to use most of them. Reading, writing, and math are skill-based subjects, particularly in kindergarten, and those skills are chosen according to specific child developmental indicators. It is likely that you will be able to use all the information in those chapters.

Each chapter provides learning activities that you can do at home with your child.

You'll find thinking skills in chapter 10 and information on assessing learning in chapter 11. The focus of chapter 12 is understanding the social environment in kindergarten, including your child's social needs and how he or she interacts with peers. Chapter 13 discusses how your child will demonstrate that he or she is prepared for moving on to the first grade. The appendixes provide information on products that meet certain kindergarten learning needs.

You won't read this book from cover to cover while lounging on the beach. I hope it will be a raggedy, dog-eared, marked-up book that has been thumbed through, spilled on, and referred to throughout the school year. Here are some tips on using this book:

Do

- Use this book as a reference guide throughout your child's kindergarten year.

- Model activities and approaches after the information you find in this book when creating your own supplemental learning activities.

- Modify the information to meet your needs and your child's needs.

Don't

- Complete the activities in this book from beginning to end. Instead, mix and match them appropriately to the curriculum and/or skills your child is learning in school.

- Use this book as a homeschool curriculum. It will help with your homeschooling in the same way it helps parents who don't homeschool—it supplements the kindergarten core curriculum.

- Challenge your child's teacher on the basis of information you find here. ("Why isn't my child covering plants and animals as it said in *Kindergarten Success?*") Instead, look for the synergy in the information from both sources.

Use this book and its resources as supplemental information to enhance your child's kindergarten curriculum—and let's make it a good year for everyone!

Getting the Most for Your Kindergartner

1

No parent says, "Oh, mediocre is okay for my child. Please do things halfway; it doesn't matter." Parents want the best for their children. This is not a matter of spending the most money on education or buying the latest educational toy. It is a matter of spending time with your child and expending effort to maximize what he or she is being provided by the school, by the community, and at home.

Getting the Most from Your School System

You wouldn't think twice about getting the most bang for your buck from a hotel, your gym, or a restaurant, and you shouldn't think twice about getting the most from your school system. The school system was designed to serve your needs, and you should take advantage of that.

Public Schools

Part of learning how to manage life as an adult is knowing how to manage interaction with bureaucratic agencies, so it makes sense that part of this learning take place within a kinder, gentler bureaucratic system. This is a good introduction to working within a system that was formed to assist in the development of children's abilities. Schools are also a workplace—with a chain of command—and that is a good induction into the workplace your child will enter as an adult. To further your child's educational experience, you will have the opportunity to meet and work with:

- School personnel: your child's teacher, teacher's aides, specialists, the school counselor, the administrator or principal, and others
- Extracurricular groups: scouts, sports, after-school programs, and community parks and recreation programs
- Parents of children from your child's class or grade level, school volunteers, and parent–teacher organizations

Participation in your child's education is paramount to his or her success. Active participation doesn't mean that you have to spend hours at the school as a volunteer, but it does include reading all of the communications your school sends either to you directly or home with your child. Also, read the school handbook and drop by your child's school on a regular basis if possible. If you can't stop by, check out the school or class Web site to see what units are being covered, any upcoming events, and so on. Participation also means attending school events when you can, going to class parties when possible, and going to parent–teacher conferences. If they are scheduled at a time when you are not available to meet, request a different time. The school administrator or principal usually requires that teachers try to accommodate your schedule.

The single most important thing you can do to get the most out of your local school system is to talk to your child's teacher. Find out what curricula your child will be covering and how you can help facilitate learning. Does the teacher see specific strengths and weaknesses that you can help enhance or bring up to speed? The teacher can help you identify your child's learning style, social skills, problem-solving abilities, and coping mechanisms.

Teachers play a role that extends outside the classroom. Your child's teacher is the perfect person to recommend systemwide and community resources. Teachers know how to find the local scout leaders, tutors, and good summer programs and community resources. Teachers are truly partners in your child's upbringing.

Your child's teacher cares about your child's well-being. Everyone has heard the stories about having a bad teacher or one who was "out to get my child." If that has been your experience, then it's even more important to have regular conversations with the teacher. Maybe his or her actions or your child's actions are being misunderstood. In any case, your child's teacher is the main source of information about school and the gateway to resources for the year, so find a way to communicate.

If you know there is a problem with the teacher that needs to be taken seriously, try the following:

- Talk to parents with children in the class ahead of your child. They may be able to tell you how the issue was approached by parents the previous year—and they will have lots to tell about their experiences with teachers your child will have next year.

- Talk to your child's principal. This may result in your child's being transferred to another class, so make sure you are prepared for that prior to making the appointment. Be willing to work with your child's current teacher prior to transferring your child. The less disruption your kindergartner experiences, the better.

- Talk to your local school administration center to see what the procedures are for transferring to another school. You will likely be required to provide transportation to a school outside your home district, but if the problem is severe enough, it will be worth it.

No matter what, active participation and communication with your child's school is essential. It empowers you to:

- Accurately monitor your child's progress
- Determine which optional activities available would enrich your child's learning experience
- Prepare your child for upcoming events, curricula, and skill introduction
- Share and add to the school learning environment
- Create a complementary learning environment in your home
- Spend time with your child

And just a word about the school secretary: this person knows more about what is going on in that building than anyone else. When I was a teacher, the school secretary always added to my success and that of my students. The secretary is a taskmaster, nurse, mom or dad, and generally just a comforting figure in what can sometimes be a really big building. The school secretary always knows what forms to fill out, which teacher is where, what students are absent and why, when the next school event is, and how much candy money you owe for the latest fund-raiser. He or she is a source of lunch money, milk money, extra pencils, bus passes, and the copy machine. Get to know and love your school secretary.

Private Schools

On a micro level, participating in your child's education if he or she attends a private school isn't much different from participating if he or she attends a public school. Private schools have access to the same community resources. If you have a child with special needs, the private school should work with the local education agencies to see that your child gets the appropriate services. Through active communication and participation, you will derive the same benefits as parents whose children attend public school.

On a macro level, private schools are different from public schools. Private schools are governed not by a school board but by an internal system. This can be both easier and harder to navigate. Dealing with private schools is easier because the schools realize that you are paying tuition every month, and they want to please their customers. Dealing with private schools is harder because they aren't accountable to the community for their actions, nor are they governed by the same due processes as the public school system. Check out the school's administration hierarchy to see how decisions are made and what roles have been created for parent governance. Also, get to know your school's secretary.

For you to really be on top of things, it's a good idea to print a copy of your state's learning standards (see chapter 4) and familiarize yourself with the topics and skills that your state thinks kindergartners should learn. You can find a copy at www.knowledgeessentials.com. Compare the standards to those of your private school's kindergarten curriculum. If the curriculum is drastically different from the required state learning standards, your child will have difficulty passing the required state assessments. If your child's curriculum meets and exceeds the standards, your child will be well served by that school.

Private schools have the flexibility to incorporate religious elements or varied teaching philosophies that public schools can't provide. They are not subject to requirements regarding the separation of church and state. Private schools operate without depending on community support (such as bond proposals); so long as their tuition-paying constituency approves of their methods and the students who graduate from the programs demonstrate success, private schools can implement teaching methods at will that fall out of the mainstream.

Getting the Most from Your Homeschool Curriculum

You are homeschooling your child because you want more control over what and how your child learns and the environment in which he or she learns it. That is admirable, but don't be fooled. To a large extent, your child's natural ability to learn certain things at certain times will dictate the way you should approach any homeschool curriculum (chapters 2 and 3 explain this more fully). The best thing you can do when starting to homeschool your child is to look at books on child development. Start with these:

- *Children's Strategies: Contemporary Views of Cognitive Development*, edited by David F. Bjorklund. Mahwah, N.J.: Erlbaum Associates, 1990.

- *Piaget's Theory: Prospects and Possibilities*, edited by Harry Beilin. Mahwah, N.J.: Erlbaum Associates, 1992.

- *Instructional Theories in Action: Lessons Illustrating Selected Theories and Models*, edited by Charles M. Reigeluth. Mahwah, N.J.: Erlbaum Associates, 1987.

- *All Our Children Learning*, Benjamin S. Bloom. New York: McGraw-Hill, 1981.

You don't have to homeschool your child all by yourself or by limiting yourself to the materials of a particular homeschool organization. Each state has some form of regional education system with centers open to the public. At your public school system's curriculum resource center, you can check out curriculum materials and supplemental materials. Most of these centers have a workroom with things like a die press that cuts out letters and various shapes, from squares to animals to holiday items. Regional education centers often provide continuing education for teachers, so they usually have some training materials on hand. Look for information about your regional center on the Web site of your State Department of Education. You can find a link to your State Department of Education at www.knowledgeessentials.com.

You can purchase homeschool curriculum kits designed to provide your child with a lion's share of the materials needed to complete a grade level. You can also buy curricula that are subject area specific. It is important to ask the company that sells the curricula to correlate the materials with your state's learning standards so that you can see which standards you need to reinforce with additional activities. You can find the companies that sell these kits at www.knowledgeessentials.com.

Using Supplemental Materials

You cannot expect any single curriculum in any public school, private school, or homeschool to meet all the learning standards for the grade level and subject area in your state. Many will meet 90 percent of the standards, and some will meet 75 percent, which is why there are supplemental materials. Schools use them, and so should you. They are simply extra materials that help your child learn more. Examples of these materials include:

- *Trade books.* These are just books that are not textbooks or workbooks—in other words, the kinds of books, fiction and nonfiction, that you would check out at the library or that your child would choose at a bookstore. Trade books don't have to tell about many things in a limited number of pages, so they can tell a lot more about a single topic than a textbook can. They give your child a chance to practice skills that he or she is learning. If you choose wisely, you can find books that use newly learned reading skills, such as blends, prefixes and suffixes, or rhyming. Sometimes these skills will be set in the context of newly learned social studies or science topics, such as weather, habitats, or your community.

Many companies provide these types of books for sale, but the most recognizable one may be Scholastic, Inc. Appendix A lists some books that are really good for kindergartners.

- *Software and the Internet.* Schools choose electronic activities and content, such as educational software and Internet sites, and electronic components, such as Leapfrog's LeapMat, allowing your child to expand his or her content knowledge while implementing skills just learned. Supplementing what your child is learning at school with these resources helps him or her gain technology skills within a familiar context. If you choose wisely, such as by starting with the software choices listed in appendix B of this book, you can sometimes enhance reading skills and/or supplement a reading or science topic while your child learns to operate a computer—talk about bang for your buck.

- *Other materials.* Videos, photographs, audio recordings, newspapers—just about anything you can find that helps expand what your child is learning is a supplemental resource. Loosely defined, supplemental resources can include a wide array of materials; your newly trained eye is limited only to what you now know is appropriate for your child.

Now you know what to do, so let's get to it.

Kindergarten Development

2

The journey begins. Good teachers base their activities on the developmental stages at which their students are performing. What is a developmental stage, and why is it important?

The ability to learn is always related to your child's stage of intellectual development. Developmental stages describe how a child thinks and learns in different growth periods. These periods are loosely defined by age but are more accurately defined by behavior. They are important because children cannot learn something until physical growth gives them certain abilities: children who are at a certain stage cannot be taught the concepts of a higher stage (Brainerd, 1978).

The theory of child development that is the basis for modern teaching was formed by Jean Piaget, who was born in 1896 in Neuchâtel, Switzerland, and died in 1980. His theories have been expanded by other educators but stand as the foundation of today's classroom.

Piaget's Stages of Cognitive Development

Piaget is best known for his stages of cognitive development. He discovered that children think and reason differently at different periods in their lives, and he believed that everyone passes through a sequence of four distinct stages in exactly the same order, but the times in which children pass through them can vary by years. Piaget also described two processes that people use from infancy through adulthood to adapt: assimilation and accommodation. *Assimilation* is the process of using the environment to place information in a category of things you know. *Accommodation* is the process of using the environment to add a new category of things you know. Both tools are implemented throughout life and can be used together to understand a new piece of information.

Okay, did you assimilate and accommodate that? The main thing Piaget tells us is that kids really can't learn certain information and skills until they reach a certain place in their growth that is determined by years and behaviors. Understanding Piaget's stages is like getting the key to Learning City because it is a behavior map that tells you what your kids are ready to learn. Let's define the stages, then look at the behaviors. Piaget's four stages of cognitive development are:

1. *Sensorimotor stage (0 to 4 years):* In this period, intelligence is demonstrated through activity without the use of symbols (letters and numbers). Knowledge of the world is limited because it is based on actual experiences or physical interactions. Physical development (mobility) allows children to cultivate new intellectual abilities. Children will start to recognize some letters and numbers toward the end of this stage.

2. *Preoperational stage (4 to 7 years):* Intelligence is demonstrated through the use of oral language as well as letters and numbers. Memory is strengthened and imagination is developed. Children don't yet think logically very often, and it is hard for them to reverse their thinking on their own. Your little angel is still pretty egocentric at this age, and that is normal.

3. *Concrete operational stage (7 to 11 years):* As children enter this stage, they begin to think logically and will begin to reverse thinking on their own—for example, they will begin to complete

inverse math operations (checking addition with subtraction, and so on). Expressing themselves by writing becomes easier. Logical thinking and expression is almost always about a concrete object, not an idea. Finally, children begin to think about other people more—they realize that things happen that affect others either more or less than they affect themselves.

4. *Formal operational stage (11 years and up):* As children become formally operational, they are able to do all the things in the concrete operational stage—but this time with ideas. Children are ready to understand concepts and to study scientific theories instead of scientific discoveries. They can learn algebra and other math concepts not represented by concrete objects that can be counted. Whereas every stage until now has continuously moved forward, this is the only stage where a step back occurs. As a teenager, your child will become egocentric once again. It won't be easy for you. Thinking and acting as if the world exists exclusively for him or her is cute behavior for a five-year-old; it is rarely cute for a teenager.

Unfortunately, only 35 percent of high school graduates in industrialized countries obtain formal operations; many people will not ever think formally. However, most children can be taught formal operations.

The graph on page 18 puts the stages in a clear perspective.

Developmental Goals for Five-Year-Olds

The first thing you need to ask yourself, as the parent of a potential kindergartner, is: "Is my child ready for school?" That depends on many things, including chronological age. But even if your child is on target chronologically speaking, it is important that he or she has also reached the following developmental milestones. A five-year-old can and will:

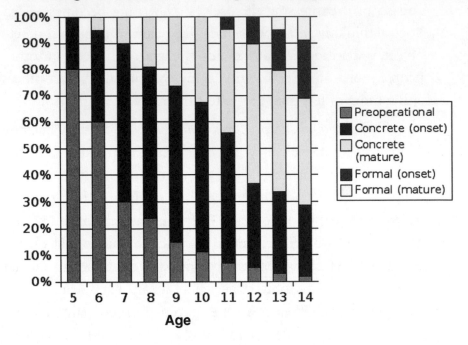

Percentage of Students in Piagetian Stages

- Verbally communicate needs, wants, and thoughts
- Use complete sentences to recount an event
- Ask questions
- Go to the bathroom by himself or herself
- Wash and dry his or her hands
- Put on and button or zip his or her own coat
- Share and take turns when playing with other children
- Separate easily from parents
- Approach new activities with enthusiasm and curiosity
- Follow two-step directions
- Run, hop, walk, skip, and throw a ball
- Hold crayons, pencils, and scissors properly

Your child needs to achieve most of the milestones on this list to be truly ready for kindergarten. Developmental variations exist, but at this critical stage, tolerance of them is more limited than at other stages. There is a threshold for acceptable behavior that includes physical and social maturity, focus, and cognitive structures that allow learning. A younger child is not likely to have all these attributes. If you are really struggling with whether your child is ready to start kindergarten, talk to your child's preschool teacher and the kindergarten teacher whom your child is likely to have if he or she starts school this year. Many times teachers can see developmental stages more easily than parents can.

Developmental Goals for Six-Year-Olds

Some, if not most, kindergartners will turn six during the school year. Here are some things you can expect from your six-year-old. A six-year-old can and will:

- Listen attentively for ten minutes or more
- Draw a picture of his or her whole self (not just a head, but a head with a neck, torso, and so on)
- Tell exactly how old he or she is and how old he or she will be next year ("I am six and a half years old; I'll be seven.")
- Think logically some of the time
- Reason
- Understand the concept of cause and effect
- Exchange best friends and enemies easily
- Exhibit bossy behavior
- Become competitive
- Become moody

- Seek adult and peer approval
- Get upset when criticized
- Learn well through active involvement
- Continue to develop fine motor skills
- Manipulate small tools, such as scissors
- Play board and card games
- Follow the rules
- Name colors
- Know his or her phone number and address
- Speak clearly

Now, you may be thinking, Oh no! My child is all over both lists! Remember, children vary greatly. It is common to find a two-and-a-half-year difference in development among children. Five- to six-year-olds who lag in specific skills often compensate by exceeding expectations in other areas of development. Don't worry. The best indicator of whether a child is in danger of falling behind is the rate of growth rather than an inventory of skills. If your child is making progress along the rough developmental continuum, don't be overly concerned about a few skills here and there.

Kindergarten Learning

3

If you write it on the chalkboard, they will learn it. Sound familiar? If you're lucky, it doesn't—but for a great majority of people it is exactly how they were taught and expected to learn. Luckily, in most schools, education has come to embrace children with different learning styles.

Learning Styles

Learning styles define how your child learns and processes information. Education experts have identified three main types of learning: visual, auditory, and physical. When learning a new math concept, for example, a visual learner will grasp the material more quickly by reading about it in a book or watching his or her teacher solve a problem on the chalkboard. An auditory learner will understand the concept if he or she can listen to the teacher explain it and then answer questions. A physical learner (also known as tactile-kinesthetic) may need to use blocks, an abacus, or other counting materials (also known as manipulatives) to practice the new concept.

If you understand that your child is a visual learner most of the time—that is, he or she is most comfortable using sight to explore the world, you can play to his or her strength and incorporate physical and auditory learning styles when appropriate. It isn't unusual to interchange learning styles for different subjects. An auditory learner can easily use kinesthetic strategies to comprehend new math concepts.

Studies have shown that accommodating a child's learning style can significantly increase his or her performance at school. In 1992, the U.S. Department of Education found that teaching to a child's learning style was one of the few strategies that improved the scores of special education students on national tests. Identifying your child's learning styles and helping him or her within that context may be the single most significant factor in your child's academic achievement. Each activity in the subject area chapters of this book lists variations that help you customize the activity to your child's learning style. Look for the symbols by the name of each learning style and use these styles to tailor the activities to your child's needs.

Learning styles are pretty easy to spot. All you have to do is watch your child's behavior when given a new piece of information.

👁 Visual

Would you give your right arm to get your child to listen to you? Are your walls a mural comprising every crayon your child has held? If you answered yes, you have a visual learner. You may not be able to get your child to choose from orally listed drive-through choices, but he or she can probably spot the sign of his favorite restaurant from miles away. Diagrams and graphs are a breeze. Your child can retell complex stories just by looking at one or two pictures from a book. Why is your child seemingly brilliant on paper and a space case when listening? Visual learners rely primarily on their sense of sight to take in information, understand it, and remember it. As long as they can see it, they can comprehend it.

Technically there are two kinds of visual learners: picture learners and print learners. Most children are a mixture of both, although some are one or the other (Willis and Hodson, 1999). Picture learners think in images; if you ask one what sound "oy" makes, he or she will likely think of a picture of a boy or a toy to remember the sounds of the letters. These kids like to draw—but you knew that by looking at your walls, right? Print learners think in language symbols: letters, numbers, and words. They would think of the actual letters "oy" to remember the sound they make together. Print learners learn to read quickly and are good spellers right off the bat. They also like to write.

Auditory

Is your child a talker? Is total silence the kiss of death to your child's concentration? Auditory learners understand new ideas and concepts best when they hear and talk about the information. If you observe a group of kids, auditory learners are the ones who learn a tune in a snap just from hearing someone sing it, or who can follow directions to the letter after being told only once or twice what to do. Some auditory learners concentrate better on a task when they have music or noise in the background, or retain new information more accurately when they talk it out. If you ask auditory learners what sound "oy" makes, they will recall the sound first and as many words as possible with that sound almost automatically.

Kinesthetic

Does your child need to touch everything? Physical learners (also known as tactile-kinesthetic learners—*tactile* for touch, *kinesthetic* for movement) use their hands or bodies to absorb new information. In some ways, everyone is a physical learner. If you peek into a classroom, you will see the physical learner tapping a pencil, finger, or foot, or twirling her hair to help her concentrate. These kids can't sit still and are in the top percentile for being diagnosed with attention deficit disorder (ADD).

Before you run to the doctor because your child can't sit still, carefully observe him over a period of time. Is the movement productive? Does he absorb or block information when moving? If he prefers to feel things in his hands or performs steady movement when trying to concentrate, he is engaging in productive learning.

Physical learners enjoy hands-on activities, such as cutting construction paper, sorting objects with their hands, and building elaborate projects. When you ask physical learners what sound "oy" makes, they will think of the physical cues they used when learning, such as tapping, physically picking the letters out of the alphabet, or holding "o" and "y" blocks.

Cognitive Learning

Cognitive learning levels are another way that teachers describe how a child processes information. I hear you saying, "Wow—how much of this do I have to remember?"—and you know I am going to say, "All of it," but it is really important. Let's recap for a minute to see how all of this fits together.

First, you learned about developmental stages, the physical growth that needs to happen before your child can learn certain things. Second, you learned about learning styles, the way your child prefers to process information. Third, you are about to learn about cognitive learning levels, the levels at which your child knows, understands, and can use information that he or she learns.

Piaget identified the developmental stages in the 1930s and 1940s. By the 1950s, a group of researchers got together, led by Benjamin Bloom, and created the cognitive learning taxonomy designed to help you understand the levels of learning that can occur with new information. Bloom is often considered one of the most important educational theorists of the twentieth century. A professor at the University of Chicago, Bloom was more than a brilliant teacher: he was a brilliant thinker. Bloom spent his career researching how thinking and learning happen in students of all ages. Bloom and his researchers broke down the learning levels as follows:

Level 1: Knowledge. The things you know—bits of information that you can memorize, such as the ABCs.

Level 2: Comprehension. The things you understand—knowing the ABCs and understanding that they represent sounds.

Level 3: Application. The things you can apply—knowing the ABCs, understanding that they represent sounds, and then sounding out a word.

Level 4: Analysis. The things that you understand well enough to think about in a new way—knowing the ABCs, understanding that they represent sounds, sounding out a word, and then figuring out what the word means.

Level 5: Synthesis. Understanding something well enough to apply it to a new situation—knowing the ABCs, understanding that they represent sounds, sounding out a word, figuring out what the word means, and using it in a new way.

Level 6: Evaluation. Understanding something so well that you can tell if it is being used correctly—knowing the ABCs, understanding that they represent sounds, sounding out a word, figuring out what the word means, using it in a new way, and figuring out if the new way is right.

Check the Bloom's Cognitive Learning Levels table on page 26 for some specific key words and behaviors for each level. Getting to know the key words will help you determine how to ask your child questions in order to find out the level at which your child understands new information. Use the examples in the right-hand column of the table to ask questions that check for each level of understanding.

Bloom's Cognitive Learning Levels

Cognitive Level	Verb	Key Words		Examples
Knowledge Recalls data. Exhibits memory of previously learned material by recalling facts and basic concepts.	Remember	choose define describe find how identify know label list match name omit outline recall	recognize reproduce select show spell state tell what when where which who why	• Defines terminology/vocabulary • Describes details and elements • Recognizes classifications and categories • Knows principles, generalizations, theories, models, and structures • Knows subject-specific skills, algorithms, techniques, and methods • Names criteria for using certain procedures • Spells words • Outlines facts, events, stories, or ideas
Comprehension Demonstrates understanding of facts and ideas by organizing, comparing, translating, interpreting, giving descriptions, and stating main ideas. Understands the meaning, translation, interpolation, and interpretation of instructions and problems.	Understand	classify compare comprehend contrast convert defend demonstrate distinguish estimate explain extend illustrate	infer interpret outline paraphrase predict relate rephrase rewrite show summarize translate	• Summarizes or retells information • Translates an equation • Outlines the main ideas • Summarizes instructions, facts, details, or other things • Compares and contrasts ideas • Explains what is happening • Identifies statements to support a conclusion • Classifies information

Bloom's Cognitive Learning Levels

Cognitive Level	Verb	Key Words		Examples
Application Solves problems in new situations by applying acquired knowledge, facts, techniques, and rules in a different way. Uses a concept in a new situation or unprompted use of an abstraction. Applies what was learned in the classroom into novel situations.	Apply	apply build change choose compute construct demonstrate develop discover identify interview manipulate	model modify operate plan predict prepare produce relate select show solve utilize	• Applies a formula to solve a problem • Uses a manual to solve a problem • Describes how to use something • Finds examples to help apply ideas, rules, steps, or an order • Describes a result • Modifies ideas, rules, steps, or an order for use in another way • Selects facts to demonstrate something
Analysis Examines and breaks information into parts by identifying motives or causes. Makes inferences and finds evidence to support generalizations. Separates material or concepts into component parts so that its organizational structure may be understood. Distinguishes between facts and inferences.	Analyze	analyze assume categorize classify compare conclusion contrast discover dissect distinction distinguish	divide examine function inference inspect list motive relationships take part in test for theme	• Troubleshoots a problem using logical deduction • Lists components or parts of a whole • Names the function of something • Makes a distinction between two or more things • Classifies or categorizes a number of things • Draws a conclusion • Lists the parts of a whole

(continued)

Bloom's Cognitive Learning Levels *(continued)*

Cognitive Level	Verb	Key Words		Examples
Synthesis Compiles information in a different way by combining elements in a new pattern or pro-posing alternative solutions. Builds a structure or pattern from diverse elements. Puts parts together to form a whole, with emphasis on creating a new meaning or structure.	Create	adapt arrange build categorize change choose combine compile compose construct create delete design develop devise discuss elaborate estimate explain formulate generate happen imagine improve	invent make up maximize minimize modify organize original originate plan predict propose rearrange reconstruct relate reorganize revise rewrite solution solve summarize suppose tell test write	• Integrates training from several sources to solve a problem • Formulates a theory • Invents a solution • Constructs a model • Compiles facts • Minimizes or maximizes an event or item • Designs a solution, model, or project • Adapts something to create another thing
Evaluation Presents and defends opinions by making judgments about information, validity of ideas, or quality of work based on a set of criteria.	Evaluate	agree appraise assess award choose compare conclude criteria	importance influence interpret judge justify mark measure opinion	• Selects the most effective solution • Explains a selection, conclusion, or recommendation • Prioritizes facts • Rates or ranks facts, characters (people), or events • Assesses the value or importance of something

Bloom's Cognitive Learning Levels

Cognitive Level	Verb	Key Words		Examples
Evaluation (continued) Makes judgments about the value of ideas or materials.		criticize decide deduct defend determine disprove dispute estimate evaluate explain	perceive prioritize prove rank rate recommend rule on select support value	• Justifies a selection, conclusion, or recommendation

Source: Adapted from Benjamin S. Bloom, *Taxonomy of Educational Objectives: The Classification of Educational Goals, by a Committee of College and University Examiners* (New York: Longmans, Green, 1956).

The Standards 4

Standards-based education came into the national spotlight over a decade ago. Communities and school districts previously made their own curriculum choices. For example, in one school district civics was taught in the eighth grade, and in another district it was taught in ninth grade, resulting in uneven and low test scores, because children were not taught the same subjects in the same grades but were tested on the same subjects.

Now, you are probably thinking, "I have *a kindergartner*, what are you talking about learning standards and test scores for?" The fact is that more than two-thirds of the states have legislatively stated learning standards and mandated assessments for kindergartners. You can find a list of the states that set learning standards and test them at www.knowledgeessentals.com. Now, let's move on to the standards.

The idea behind the standards reform movement is straightforward: when states set clear standards defining what a child should know and be able to do in certain grades, teachers and learners are able to focus their efforts and highlight particular areas in which they need improvement. Ideally, the standards show teachers what they need to teach by allowing curricula and assessments that measure performance to be aligned with the standards.

As with all reform movements, there are people who disagree with the idea of creating common learning standards. They primarily point to tendencies to simply "teach the test" and complain that the standards limit content breadth and community input. The real gripe may lie in the fact that education has always been a local issue. It is easy to fear change when you fear that community values may be lost by standardizing state curriculum. Others believe that standards even the playing field. Before you form your own opinion, let's take a look at standards-based education.

Standards-based education lists content and skills that children need to learn at each grade level. Success depends on combining content and performance standards with consistent curriculum and instruction as well as appropriate assessment and accountability.

This is the point where teachers and learners start to feel anxious. Everything sounds very official, particularly the accountability part. What does this language mean, and what happens if children don't meet learning standards requirements?

Relax—there are no learning standards police patrolling our neighborhood schools, libraries, and bookstores. There are simply baselines by which the state determines eligibility for a high school diploma.

Let's start by defining learning standards.

Types of Learning Standards

Learning standards are broad statements that describe what content a child should know and what skills a child should be able to do in different subject areas.

Content standards are a form of learning standards that describe the topics to be studied, not the skills to be performed.

Performance standards are a form of learning standards that describe the skills to be performed, not the content to be studied.

Public school teachers must ensure that their students are taught the required content and skills because they are accountable not only to the students but also to their state, their school district, and their community for every child's performance on test scores. Private schools are accountable to their constituency with respect to student performance but not to the public. In fact, school requirements as well as teacher licensure are not as strictly monitored for private schools. The academically strong private schools institute internal standards that meet or exceed state expectations for public schools, but there are private schools that feel that other aspects of child development, such as religious development, take precedence over academics. If your child attends private school, you must research the school to make sure it meets your expectations both academically and socially.

The use of testing to change classroom instruction is central to the theory of standards-based reform. It assumes that educators and the public can agree on what should be taught; that a set of clear standards can be developed, which in turn drive curriculum and instruction; and that tests can measure how well students perform in terms of those standards. There are two main types of standardized testing that your child will encounter:

1. Tests to determine individual student eligibility for promotion and graduation, college admission, or special honors. This type of testing has a long history. Examples include high school exit exams and college entrance exams, such as the Scholastic Aptitude Test (SAT) and Advanced Placement (AP) tests.

2. Tests that measure and compare school, school district, statewide, and national performance for broad public accountability. Increasingly, policy makers at the federal, state, and local levels want to identify ways to measure student performance in order to see how well the public education system is doing its job. The goals of this accountability approach include providing information about the status of the educational system, motivating desired

change, measuring program effectiveness, and creating systems for financially sanctioning schools and requiring educators to receive more training based on the performance of their students.

It makes sense for you to ensure that the content and the skills you work on with your child match the content and skills that the state has identified for that grade level. Children will do better on the standardized tests when more learning standards match assessment, or test, requirements. Legislation is in place that requires states to align their learning expectations with their testing expectations. The disconnect came when federal requirements for learning standards preceded testing requirements. Many states took the opportunity to test for content and skills that seemed more important than the ones enumerated in the learning standards. States and schools are working under federal guidelines to make all of the content match in a few years.

Learning Standards Resources

Each state has created a document that describes what children are supposed to know about and what they are supposed to be able to do at each grade level and in each subject area. You may wonder who writes the standards and why you should believe that these people know what is best. A lot of public school teachers have wondered the same thing.

You can rest assured that writing the state learning standards is a collaborative effort. Most states rely on input from experts who know about the grade level and subject area. These experts could include teachers, researchers, people from the education industry, and school administrators. In an endnote or footnote, each document lists the people hired by the state to help write the final version.

You can locate the standards that apply to your child through your State Department of Education's Web site, by calling your State Department of Education, or through the Internet at www.knowledgeessentials.com.

There are several things you should read for:

1. *Content standards:* What topics will your child be studying?

2. *Performance standards:* What skills must your child develop by the end of the year?

3. *Resources:* What resources are designed to help teachers meet the learning standards? Can you access them?

4. *Correlation reports:* Does the state provide a listing of how the required textbooks and other materials meet their own learning standards? Your school district should also be able to provide you with this information.

As you read your state's learning document, you may notice that you don't always agree with what is listed for your child to be learning. Is there anything you can do?

If your child attends a public school, there is little you can do to protest the prescribed curricula, but you can certainly enhance the curricula through learning activities at home. If your child attends a private school, you may have greater influence over classroom activities (as a paying customer), but you will probably not get the curricula changed to meet your concerns.

If you teach your child at home, then you have as much control as you would like over your child's curricula. You undoubtedly have specific beliefs that have led you to decide to homeschool, and you can remain true to those beliefs while still covering the required curricula. Even if you don't believe the required curricula are entirely appropriate, the assessments required by the states and higher education institutions will be normed to the learning standards of the state in which you live. The standards are just the basics that your child will need to succeed in mainstream society. There are many more opportunities for learning across a wide range of subjects that can be totally up to you.

Kindergarten Reading

Beginning of Kindergarten Reading Checklist

Students who are working at the standard level at the beginning of kindergarten:

____ Recognize signs and symbols in the environment

____ Associate sounds with letters

____ Recognize their first name

____ Hold a book the correct way and turn the pages from front to back

____ Can retell favorite stories

I bet you can't wait for your child to begin reading. It is a major step in his or her development and something that will foster learning for a lifetime. Most five-year-olds are able to recognize common logos, such as McDonald's golden arches or the brand name on their favorite box of cookies. Your child will begin to recognize his or her own first name. He or she will also begin to identify words such as "exit," "enter," "men," "women," and "stop." These are words that are frequently found in your child's environment. All of these things indicate that your child has begun to associate words with print, which begins the process of reading. Your child will probably begin reading written words somewhere between the ages of four and seven years of age.

In kindergarten, reading readiness skills are taught in all aspects of the curriculum. Listening skills, vocabulary building, imagination development, and cognitive skills are reading readiness skills. Your child will begin to understand that things can be organized by classification and categorization, such as by size, color, and shape.

Reading can be a complicated process because there is so much for a child to remember; however, most children do learn to read. Some children learn quickly; others take more time. It is important not to compare your child to others. Applaud your child's efforts and successes and encourage him or her to keep trying. Keep in mind that your child is starting from scratch, and there's so much to learn! Patience will bring out confidence.

You can help your child with reading by reading to him or her daily and discussing the stories. This is the single most important thing you can do to prepare your child for success in reading. This is a habit that you may have begun very early in your child's life, but if not, it's never too late to start. There's nothing better than sharing a good bedtime story with your child. It will be something for both of you to look forward to at the end of a busy day. Reading aloud to your child is a wonderful way to aid in oral language development and to increase his or her knowledge of the world. Reading aloud helps develop a concept of print and a sense of story.

Phonemic Awareness

Phonemic awareness is one important component of the kindergarten reading program. Phonemic awareness simply means knowing the sounds that letters of the alphabet make. Specific skills your child will need to learn are naming the letters and their sounds, left-to-right progression, beginning letters of words, ending letters of words, rhyme, syllables, segmentation, and blending. These skills are usually presented through word play.

For young children, reading is a physical act as well as a mental one. It involves hand-eye coordination. Your child will learn that words go across the page from left to right and top to bottom and that the words on a page are made up of letters and are separated by a space. He or she will also learn that each letter has at least two forms: one for capital letters and one for lowercase letters. Your child will understand that the words on a page have meanings. When he or she is able to connect all this information, that is when he or she learns to read.

The following table describes some important skills related to phonemic awareness, where children run into problems, and what you can do to help them along.

Phonemic Awareness Skills	Having Problems?	Quick Tips
Understands directionality and the concept of print	Has problems following the print left to right, top to bottom, and front to back	Give your child the opportunity to turn the pages as you read a book of high interest. Talk about the title and illustrator and show your child the parts of the book that contain the title and the name of the illustrator. Discuss the illustrations on each page before you begin to read. Point to the words that you read; reread the page as your child points to the words.
Develops letter knowledge	Has problems recognizing letters and associating sounds with the letters	When you drive your child places, find particular letters. Spend about five minutes daily using alphabet flash cards. Using old coloring books as worksheets, ask your child to find a letter and circle it every time it is on the page. Using old magazines and scissors, go through the ads and cut out words that begin with a particular letter. Set up an alphabet corner in your house. Stock it with materials to make letters (pipe cleaners, glue, stencils), letters to trace, plastic letters for word building, alphabet stamps, alphabet puzzles, and alphabet books. Spend time in this area with your child.
Blends and segments words	Has problems sounding out words	Make letter play a fun activity for your child. Begin using two-letter words and practice putting the sounds together. When your child can blend two sounds, begin to practice with three-letter words that have the same vowel sounds (for example, "man," "can," "fan," "tan"). Provide the ending sounds and ask your child to try various beginning sounds until he or she makes a real word.

Phonemic Awareness Activities

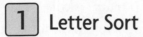 **Letter Sort**

TIME: 15 minutes

MATERIALS

■ set of letters (plastic letters, ABC flash cards, or make your own out of heavy paper)

■ poster paper with two large circles drawn on it

Learning happens when: you call out letters to your child and ask him to sort the letters into two groups. One group will be letters that are in his name; the other will consist of letters that are not in his name. Have your child put the letters onto the circles that are drawn on the poster paper. Some additional sorting choices are: letters that have curves versus letters that are all straight, letters that have tails versus letters that do not, and letters with circles versus letters without circles. When your child sorts the letters into groups, have him explain why he placed each letter in each group.

Variations: Using a set of capital and lowercase letters, ask your child to sort capital letters versus lowercase letters. You could also use magnetic letters and group them onto various objects that are magnetic, such as a refrigerator.

👁 Visual learners look at the ways the letters are alike and different but may also need to see the word that you are saying written down. Your child can draw a picture about the word or trace the word after you write it.

✋ Kinesthetic learners focus on the physical act of moving the letters into two groups. Ask your child to clap when he finishes sorting or slap his hand down on the circle containing the letters that he finished sorting.

👂 Encourage auditory learners to describe the shapes of the letters and to say their names as they are sorting. Ask your child to say the individual sounds of the letters too.

Mastery occurs when: your child can group the letters in three different ways and explain his reasons for the groupings.

You may want to help your child a little more if: he is unable to sort the letters and give a reasonable explanation for his choices.

2 Letter Match Concentration Game

Learning happens when: your child plays Concentration and matches the letters as you play. You remember how to play this, right? Lay two of the same letters face down and then ask your child to draw a card. Ask your child to draw a second card and if it matches then he has a set. If it doesn't match then he should put both cards back and try to remember what letters they were and where they were located so that he can use them to make a match on another turn. Be sure to model thinking aloud by naming each letter and the sound it makes.

TIME: 15 minutes

MATERIALS
▪ two sets of letters (you can buy ABC flash cards or make your own out of heavy paper or index cards)

Variations: Use two sets of letters, capital and lowercase.

- 👁 Visual learners will like looking for the matching letters, and you can enhance the visual cues by writing the letter on a dry erase board or on paper instead of (or while) saying the letter you want your child to match.

- ✋ Your child will really like adding a step to this game, such as hopping in place when she makes a match or racing to another spot to lay the matched pair of letters down in a designated space.

- 👂 Auditory learners will like saying the name and sound of the letters. Take this activity a step further by asking your child to say a word that begins with the same letters she matched.

Mastery occurs when: your child can match most of the letters and identify the sound each letter makes.

You may want to help your child a little more if: she is unable to identify many letter matches and their letter sounds.

3   Letters and Words

TIME: 20–25 minutes

MATERIALS
- old magazine or coloring book
- safety scissors
- glue
- 12 × 18-inch (or larger) sheet of construction paper
- marker

Fold the paper into thirds lengthwise and label the three columns Picture, Beginning Letter, and Word. You can also find a table to print at www.knowledgeessentials.com.

Learning happens when: you and your child create a poster. Have your child cut ten pictures of living things out of old magazines or coloring books. Then he will glue the first picture onto the first column on the paper as he tells you its name. You will write the beginning letter in the second column and say the letter's name with the sound it makes. In the third column write the word that names the picture. After you demonstrate this two or three times, allow your child to provide more of the information that you write.

- 👁 Visual learners like finding the pictures and making the chart, and you can enhance the activity by asking your child to outline the word you wrote. Outlining the word helps your child identify the shapes of the word, which is the first step to being able to tell if a word "looks right" when trying to spell.

- ✋ Kinesthetic learners will like cutting and pasting pictures. Make more of an impact by cutting and pasting letters too. If your child glues a picture of a cat on the poster, ask him to glue a "C" in the column for the beginning letter.

- 👂 Auditory learners will enjoy giving you the directions on what to write during this activity. Further the impact by discussing the letters and sounds that correspond to the pictures and asking him to tell you about the pictures he finds.

Mastery occurs when: your child can write the beginning sound and the word that represents each picture.

You may want to help your child a little more if: he can't identify the beginning sounds of the words as well as write the word that names the picture.

4 Blending Sounds

Write a consonant on each side of the cube with a marker. You might want to have more than one cube so that you can have more consonants. Write the same two letters beginning with a vowel and ending with a consonant (for example, "it," "un," "et") six times on the piece of paper, as shown in the chart. You can also find lists such as this to print at www.knowledgeessentials.com.

TIME: 15 minutes

MATERIALS
- small cube(s) (wood or foam)
- pencil
- marker
- paper

____at
____at
____at
____at
____at
____at

Learning happens when: your child rolls the cube like a die, reads the letter on top, then writes the letter from the die in front of one group of letters on the paper and blends the letters to read the word. For example, if the two letters on the paper are "it" and your child rolls an "s," she makes and reads the word "sit." Repeat the procedure until your child has six words that make sense.

Variations: Do this same activity but write consonant-vowel combinations on the paper and have your child roll the die to get ending letters. You say the sounds as you put the letters together to form a word, and your child reads the word.

- 👁 Visual learners focus on the way the letters look together to form a word. Ask your child to outline the word in her favorite color.
- ✋ Kinesthetic learners will like rolling the die and writing the letters. If any of the words your child makes is a verb (for example, "run," "sit," "pat," "hop") ask your child to do what the word says. You might say from the start that you won't do "hit."
- 👂 Auditory learners will like saying the letters, sounds, and words. When the word list is complete, ask your child to say each word and see how many of them rhyme.

Mastery occurs when: your child can make three-letter words out of the letters she has rolled combined with the letters that were written on the paper, and read them to you.

You may want to help your child a little more if: she is unable to read any three-letter words. Make the sounds as she puts the letters together before asking your child to do it on her own.

5   Building Words

Learning happens when: your child listens as you say a three-letter word, then moves the poker chips into place to build that word.

Variations: Ask your child to write the letters on paper after he has built the word with poker chips.

- 👁 Enhance your visual learner's experience by asking him to draw a picture about one of the words.
- ✋ Kinesthetic learners respond well to pointing to the letter when saying its sound.
- 👂 Auditory learners always like saying the letters, sounds, and words, so ask your child to name another word that sounds like the word he spelled.

Mastery occurs when: your child can use the poker chips to spell the three-letter words that you say to him.

You may want to help your child a little more if: he is unable to spell the words that you have given him.

TIME: 15 minutes

MATERIALS
▪ poker chips with letters written on them (three chips for each word on your list)
▪ list of three-letter words (you can find one at www. knowledgeessentials.com)

6   Hat Trick

Cut the construction paper into twenty-six rectangles. Write one letter of the alphabet on each rectangle. Place all the letters into the hat.

Learning happens when: your child draws a letter out of the hat and says the name of the letter, the sound the letter makes, and a word that begins with that letter. Repeat the procedure until all the letters have been used.

TIME: 15 minutes

MATERIALS
▪ hat
▪ construction paper
▪ marker

Variations: Ask your child to say a word that ends with the letter she drew or a word that has the letter anywhere in it.

- 👁 Visual learners get more out of this activity if they write the word on paper so they can see it.
- ✋ Kinesthetic learners connect with drawing the letters out of the hat. Add to the enjoyment by letting your child act out a word that begins with that letter.
- 👂 Extend the activity for an auditory learner by asking her to tell you long vowel and short vowel sounds. When she draws a consonant from the hat, see if she can use that letter in a blend (for example, "st," "ch," "tr," "pl").

Mastery occurs when: your child is able to come up with all the letter names and sounds and can name a word that begins with each letter.

You may want to help your child a little more if: she can't identify more than five to ten letters and sounds and think of a word to go with each letter.

Comprehension

Remember how excited you were when your child said his or her first word? Then he or she said a word and actually knew what it meant. Now it's time for your child to go a step further. He or she will be able to read words and understand what they mean.

Comprehension is an essential component in every reading program. Comprehension means understanding and remembering what is read. Studies show that good readers activate prior knowledge, create visual images, make inferences to draw conclusions, ask questions, determine important ideas, and synthesize what they have read. Teaching comprehension involves modeling and explaining strategies to your child, giving him or her guided practice (in which more responsibility for the task is gradually given to the child), and finally encouraging independent practice.

You can model reading a story by reading slowly out loud and pausing occasionally to think out loud about the story. Point to each word as you read it. When you've finished, reread the story. You may want to ask predictive questions ("What might happen next?"), discuss the meanings of a word, or ask your child to retell the story. Talking about the story helps your kindergartner make a personal connection to it,

Sight Words

Phonics skills first result in your child knowing a set of sight words, or words that are so common that your child immediately recognizes them without sounding them out. Some sight words ("I," "if," "he," "as") are obviously appropriate for first graders; others ("could," "know," "think," "where") are not. Most educators use the Dolch list of sight words for beginning readers. The Dolch high-frequency list was published by Edward William Dolch, Ph.D., in his book *Problems in Reading* (Garrard Press, 1948). The Dolch list of high-frequency words comprises 220 words—excluding nouns—that were common to the word lists of the International Kindergarten Union, the Gates list, and the Wheeler-Howl list—lists that were used in beginning reading programs in the 1940s. The Dolch list has held up over time as a reliable high-frequency word list for beginning reading programs. Some words are out of date but not many. You can find the Dolch list at www.knowledgeessentials.com.

Many students do not need extra practice with sight words, as they learn them by reading them repeatedly in context. The learning of sight words in isolation does not make a reader. Sometimes a student can read the words from a list and not recognize the same words in a book or story. Sight words are an important component of early reading, not the basis for it.

Your child will be expected to recognize certain sight words and to sound out one-syllable words. Not all one-syllable words are sight words. Sight words are determined by frequency of use as well as how difficult they are to read. One-syllable words are just short words that are naturally the first words your child should start reading.

Comprehension Skills	Having Problems?	Quick Tips
My child remembers every detail of a story.	Can't discuss the main ideas from the story	Begin to use self-monitoring strategies. Choose stories that are of interest to your child. Ask your child one simple question after reading each page.
My child remembers events in order.	Can't recall the sequence of events in the story	Retell the story by "reading" the illustrations. Sequence the main ideas by telling what happened first, second, and last. Discuss the sequence of your child's morning. "What happened first, brushing your teeth or getting out of bed?" "Did you then get on the school bus or get dressed?"
My child recognizes words that are difficult to sound out.	Has problems recognizing common high-frequency sight words	Find a list of frequently used sight words for kindergartners at www.knowledgeessentials.com. Use this list for activities you can do every day with your child. Make flash cards, use six to eight cards at a time, and vary your activities. Occasionally ask your child to use these sight words in a sentence. Write six to eight words on a piece of paper, hold up a flash card, and say the word. Ask your child to find that word on the list and underline it with a blue crayon. Continue in this manner until all words have been located on the list. Also try asking your child to read the words to you. When your child recognizes these six to eight words, choose another set from the list.
My child draws conclusions from inferences.	Has problems making inferences about the story	Relate the inference to your child, using such questions as "What would you do?" "If you do that, what would happen then?" Read the next page and then compare what really happened in the story to what your child said. Observe the details in the illustrations and use the thinking aloud process to talk about them. Ask questions about the illustrations, then read the story and compare it to the predictions your child made based on the illustrations.
My child listens for information.	Has problems recalling the details of stories	Pick a story that interests your child and read it to him or her, stopping after each page to ask questions about the details. After your child answers, reread the sentence that contains the answer.

promotes language development, and gives you insight into your child's comprehension.

Kindergarten reading begins your child's first formal instruction in reading. He or she will begin by learning and practicing skills through the use of texts that have rhyme, rhythm, repetition, and everyday language. Illustrations match the text, and text placement is consistent on the page. Repetitive sequences introduce simple one-word changes. Examples of text that foster independent emergent reading are big books; patterned, predictable books; and rebus books.

During this phase of reading, you should not expect total accuracy. After hearing and discussing the story and the illustrations, your child should begin to "read" the story using the pictures as clues. This pretend "reading" is an important stage called emergent reading. Your child should locate the front and back of a book, the title and title page, the top and bottom of a page, and where to begin reading. The table on the facing page describes some important skills that enable reading comprehension, some problems your child might encounter, and some quick tips on how you can help.

Comprehension Activities

1 Emergent Story Reading

Learning happens when: you go through the book and discuss each picture with your child. Next, read the entire book out loud, including the title of the book and the author's name, and point to each word as you go along. Finally, reread the story, stopping at predictable places, and ask your child to fill in the words that you skip.

Variations: Have your child "read" the pictures on each page to retell the story.

TIME: 15 minutes

MATERIALS
book with predictability or repetition, such as *Brown Bear* or *There Was an Old Lady Who Swallowed a Fly*

👁 Visual learners are good at reading the pictures. Try asking your child to copy words from the book into a separate note-book or to draw a picture that describes something that wasn't illustrated in the book.

✋ Kinesthetic learners often need to touch the pictures as you discuss them. A good technique is to ask, "Can you find . . . in the pictures?" Let your child touch the page to indicate the "find." He'll also like to turn the pages for you.

👂 An auditory learner will like to talk about the picture, so ask him to read along with you by repeating what you say as you read.

Mastery occurs when: your child fills in the correct words that you skip and can predict what happens next in the story.

You may want to help your child a little more if: he can't remember the predictable words or can't predict what happens next.

2 | Inferring Characters' Traits

TIME: 20 minutes

MATERIALS
- storybook
- large piece of paper
- marker

Learning happens when: you read the book out loud with your child. After reading the book, ask these questions: "Who is the main character? What is he or she like?" "Who else is important in the story? How does the main character feel about them? How can you tell?" "How does each minor character feel about the main character?" Make a character web using the answers your child provides. The figure here is an example of a character web that tells about Clifford, the Big Red Dog.

Variations: Go back through the book when you ask the questions and let your child look at the pictures as she is answering the questions. Do the same activity using several different books.

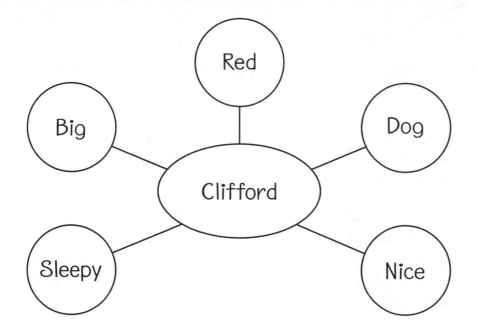

👁 Let your visual learner color in the circles of the character web or draw a picture that shows what she described in the character web.

✋ Let your kinesthetic learner turn the pages as you read the book, and ask her to point at each character in the pictures.

👂 Auditory learners should extend the description of the character by telling you more about that character. Encourage your child to imagine what she thinks the character would do in situations or locations that you think of and are not in the book.

Mastery occurs when: your child can answer who, why, what, where, and how questions about the characters.

You may want to help your child a little more if: she can't answer all the questions. Let her look at the pictures for clues to answer the question.

3 | Problem/Solution

TIME: 15 minutes

MATERIALS
■ *Goldilocks and the Three Bears*

Read or tell the story to your child.

Learning happens when: your child can identify problems from the story, such as trespassing on private property, and brainstorm ideas about how to solve them. Compare your child's solution to the problem to what happens in the book.

Variations: Help other fairy tale characters with their problems. How might Jack improve his financial lot without having to steal from or slay the giant? How could two of the Little Pigs have avoided going to the third brother for shelter and safety from the wolf?

👁 Visual learners can make their own ending to the story by drawing a picture to illustrate their solution.

✌ Kinesthetic learners can make puppets for each main character in the story using old socks or brown paper lunch bags. Have your child tell his version of the fairy tale using the puppets.

👂 This activity is already great for auditory learners, but they'll also enjoy telling their own version of the fairy tale.

Mastery occurs when: your child can identify the main problems in the story and tell how he would solve them.

You may want to help your child a little more if: he can't identify the main problem in each story. Reread the story and ask your child questions to lead him to the main problem.

4   Practicing Predictions

TIME: 25 minutes

MATERIALS
■ picture book (see Appendix A for suggestions)
■ sticky notes

Learning happens when: you tell your child she will practice making predictions about stories by looking at the illustrations. Begin by showing the front cover and discussing the details of the illustration. Turn to the first page of illustrations and ask your child what is happening in the story. Quickly jot down what your child says on a sticky note and place it on the corresponding page. Do this page by page for the whole book and spend time listening to your child predict the story. When finished, read the book out loud and peel the sticky notes off each page. Ask your child leading questions to help her compare her version of the story to the actual story.

Variations: If this is difficult for your child, make predictions about the illustrations on one page at a time, and gradually add more pages as she becomes more comfortable with the activity. Use the same procedure with a variety of books.

- 👁 Visual learners enjoy illustrations and will be able to provide more detail about the story from the pictures than other learners will. Extend the skill by asking your child to tell you what pictures should be in the story but aren't. Let your child draw the pictures that should be in the story.

- ✋ Kinesthetic learners will enjoy turning the pages and pulling the sticky notes off the words. Ask your child to act out what happens either before or after one or two of her favorite pictures.

- 👂 Auditory learners will enjoy talking about the pictures. Ask her to tell you what each character in the picture should be saying.

Mastery occurs when: your child makes reasonable predictions about the story based on the illustrations and compares the actual story to her predictions.

You may want to help your child a little more if: she is unable to make a reasonable prediction from looking at the illustrations. Model the expected behavior for your child and ask why she thinks you made that prediction.

5 Fact or Fiction

TIME: 20–25 minutes

MATERIALS
■ two books with similar themes, one fiction and one nonfiction, such as *Lisa in New York* and *L Is for Liberty, Marsupial Sue* and *Pockets That Hop,* or *A Day at the Airport* and *Amazing Airplanes*

Learning happens when: you read two books to your child on the same theme, one fiction and one nonfiction. Talk about the similarities and differences in the two books and have your child identify which book is fiction and which is nonfiction.

Variations: Select six books (three fiction and three nonfiction) and have your child sort a stack of books into categories of fiction and nonfiction.

👁 Visual learners will enjoy looking at the books to sort them. They may also notice some differences in the way the story is organized. Ask your child to draw one thing about each book that tells if the book is fiction or nonfiction.

✋ Kinesthetic learners will enjoy moving the books to sort and categorize them, as they talk about the stories. Ask him to look through the books and put sticky notes on the things that help him know the book is fiction or nonfiction.

👂 Auditory learners will like to talk about the similarities and differences in the stories. Ask your child to tell you a little about each book that makes him know whether the book is fiction or nonfiction.

Mastery occurs when: your child can listen to a story and then decide whether it is fact or fiction.

You may want to help your child a little more if: he can't sort the books into fact or fiction.

6 | Beginning, Middle, and End

Divide the paper into three sections and label them Beginning, Middle, and End.

Learning happens when: you read the book with your child. For each section, have your child draw and color a picture of an event that happened in the book.

Variations: Ask your child to describe each event she drew. Write down your child's description below each picture.

- 👁 Visual learners benefit from seeing the pictures they have created for the beginning, middle, and end. Challenge your visual learner by asking her to draw more parts of the story in frames like a comic strip.
- ✋ For your kinesthetic learner, cut the pictures apart, mix them up, and ask her to put them in order again.
- 👂 Ask your auditory learner to tell you about her drawing.

Mastery occurs when: your child can choose an event to draw and color that accurately represents that section of the story.

You may want to help your child a little more if: she chooses all events from one section of the book instead of from all three sections.

TIME: 25 minutes

MATERIALS
- picture book (see Appendix A for suggestions)
- paper
- crayons
- marker

Environmental Learning

Take advantage of your everyday environment. There are many chances throughout the day to help your child learn to read.

When you and your child are on your way to school or home, ask him or her what words he or she recognizes on the signs around your town. Talk about each one and ask your child what letters are in each word. What is the beginning sound or ending sound? Have your child find words that begin with the same letter as his or her name. At dinner asks questions about what your child did during the day: "Did you do that at the beginning, middle, or end of the day?" "What was your favorite part of the day? Why was it your favorite?" "How did it make you feel?"

Your child will be able to develop reading readiness skills as you make time to ask questions about the world around you. It will also be valuable quality time your child will enjoy.

End of Kindergarten Reading Skills Checklist

Students who are working at the standard level at the end of kindergarten:

____ Know words have meanings

____ Know letters make words

____ Know all or part of the alphabet

____ Know most of the sounds each letter makes

____ Recognize familiar written words, such as their name

____ Recognize written words found in their daily environment

Kindergarten Writing 6

Have you been waiting for the day when your child starts writing on paper instead of everything else? That day is here, my friend. Kindergarten is the first formal training your child will receive in reading and writing.

Reading and writing fit together as perfectly as bacon and eggs. In school, reading and writing are always taught together because they go hand in hand. For the first few years of your child's formal education, you will barely be able to separate the two—all reading activities will involve writing activities, and vice versa.

Kindergarten writing is an active learning process that involves interaction with other students and working with various utensils your child will enjoy, including brushes, markers, chalk, crayons, pens, and pencils. He or she will experience writing on a variety of surfaces, such as paper, chalkboards, dry erase boards, clay, and sandpaper.

Beginning of Kindergarten Writing Checklist

Students who are working at the standard level at the beginning of kindergarten:

—— Have control over hand movements

—— Are interested in writing

—— Play-write with scribbles

—— Draw pictures

—— Hold crayons and other writing implements

—— Associate writing with communicating wants and needs

Writing Readiness

Children prepare to learn to write by using a variety of activities that require hand-eye coordination and the use of small muscles. Playing with pegboards, beads, pattern blocks, lacing cards, clay, puzzles, scissors, glue, paints, and crayons uses the same muscles as writing. Kindergarten curriculum for writing includes activities that help strengthen these small muscles. For example, if your child's class is studying the letter "m," the teacher is likely to introduce the letter with activities, such as cutting out pictures of words that begin with the letter "m," gluing colored macaroni onto "m" shapes, and sorting M&Ms by color. Materials would include letter "m" stamps and stamp pad, templates to trace the letter "m," and markers and paper. Although not all of these activities involve writing, they help build small muscles in the hands and improve hand-eye coordination.

Writing Readiness Skills	Having Problems?	Quick Tips
Understands directionality, the concept that print goes from left to right, and from top to bottom	Makes letters backwards or may write entire word backwards	Don't worry about it! It is developmentally appropriate for your child to do this. He just needs more experience with print and print concepts. Modeling correct direction when writing for him is the easiest thing you can do to help. You can also think aloud and talk about writing as you write for him. (For example: "This is where we start to write our names; names start with capital letters; your name starts with C, and then comes h. . . .")
Gains increasing control in penmanship, such as pencil grip, paper position, and beginning stroke	Can write, but does not form letters properly	Again, this is a developmental trait that can be addressed with more exposure to play with very small toys, such as clay, play dough, and so on. This will help build small muscles in your child's hands.

Writing Readiness Activities

1 Letter Die Game

Before you begin you will need to write a letter on each side of the cube with a marker. Prepare the graph paper by drawing eleven rows. In the bottom row of each column, write one of the letters from each side of the die. An example of a graph is shown here.

Learning happens when: your child tosses the die, reads the letter, and writes the letter in the corresponding column. The first letter to get to the top of the column wins!

TIME: 15 minutes

MATERIALS
- wooden or foam cube
- graph paper with six columns
- marker

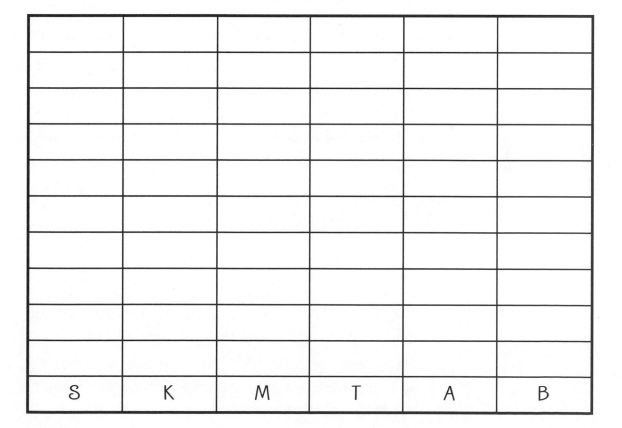

Variations: Make a die with capital letters. Play the game by asking your child to write the matching lowercase letters, or vice versa.

👁 Visual learners can lightly color the columns different colors before they start rolling the die to add greater visual distinction to the activity.

✋ Kinesthetic learners will particularly like the action of throwing the die and writing the letters in the grid. Add more activity by placing crayons and paper on the other side of the room. When a letter makes it to the top of the grid, ask your child to run to the paper and write down the letter that made it to the top of the grid first.

👂 Ask your auditory learner to say a word that starts with the letter each time he rolls the die.

Mastery occurs when: your child can identify each letter and write it correctly.

You may want to help your child a little more if: he struggles to name the letters or write them correctly. Concentrate on just a few letters at a time and then move on to others. Try making a dotted version of each letter in the graph for your child to trace.

2 Personalized Writing

TIME: 20 minutes

MATERIALS
▪ photos of family
▪ paper
▪ glue
▪ pencil or marker

Before you start the activity:

1. Write the name of each person on the top of a sheet of paper using a dotted line. You are going to let your child trace the dotted line to make the letters in the name.

2. Underneath the dotted-line name, write the name dotted again, but use fewer dots—this time it is more like connecting the dots than tracing.

3. Underneath the connect-the-dots version of the name, draw a blank line so your child can write the name on her own.

Learning happens when: your child picks up the picture of a family member, says that person's name, makes the beginning sound, and locates a page containing the family member's name. She can then glue the picture onto the page, trace the person's name, connect the dots to make the name, and then write the name. Repeat until all pictures and words are matched.

Variations: Ask your child to tell you what she likes about each person or to tell you about a happy memory with this family member. Let your child dictate a sentence about each person as you write it. Staple the pages together to make a book. Keep the book so that your child can reread it.

- 👁 Ask your visual learner to put the pictures in order by age or to group the pictures by immediate family (such as your family, your sister's family, Grandma and Grandpa) or by events, such as vacations, holidays, or sports.

- ✋ Let your kinesthetic learner act out one of the events in the pictures.

- 👂 Encourage your auditory learner to say the name of each family member she identifies, speak each letter as she writes, and talk about each person.

Mastery occurs when: your child has matched all the pictures to the correct names and then writes the names.

You may want to help your child a little more if: she is not able to match each picture to the correct name. Start with fewer choices and add more as your child masters the first set.

3   Describe a Toy

TIME: 15 minutes

MATERIALS
- one of your child's toys
- small pieces of paper
- sheet of lined paper
- marker

Before you begin, write one adjective on each small piece of paper. Diversify the adjectives with ones that describe the toy and others that do not. Prepare the sheet of lined paper with five sentence frames about the toy (for example, "My bear is _____.")

Learning happens when: your child identifies the adjectives that describe his toy and copies the correct adjectives into the sentence frames. Read the sentences out loud together.

Variations: Use different objects and repeat the same process with adverbs and sentence frames.

- 👁 Ask your visual learner to draw pictures of other items the adjective describes.
- ✋ Say an adjective and ask your kinesthetic learner to go find the toy it describes, bring it back to you, and complete the sentence frame.
- 👂 Auditory learners should discuss and describe the toy.

Mastery occurs when: your child can complete the sentences with adjectives that describe the object.

You may want to help your child a little more if: he is unable to complete the sentences with adjectives that describe each object.

4 | ABC Book

Learning occurs when: you pick a consonant to use in this activity, for example, "Bb." Discuss the sound "Bb" makes and say three or four "Bb" words. Ask your child if she knows any "Bb" words. Write the words on a sheet of paper. Make a template for both the uppercase and lowercase consonants and ask your child to trace both onto the paper. Now decorate the letters using any of the art materials that she chooses. Make a blank line below each word for later use. Reread the list when finished.

This should be an ongoing project that you periodically revisit until all twenty-six letters have been made. Save and date the letters from each session and also save the list of words. Alphabetize the pages to make an ABC book. In time your child should want to write the words in the blank lines. You can make the project last a few months. The finished product will show you and your child how much progress she has made in writing. This is an excellent learning tool and a wonderful keepsake.

Variations: Try this with numbers! Write a number on the sheet of paper, but this time ask your child to find pictures that contain the same number of items as the number on the page. Ask your child to glue the picture on the page, then write the number under the picture.

👁 Your visual learner can draw pictures of things that start with each letter in her book.

✋ Involve your kinesthetic learner in every part of the activity, including setting up and cleaning up.

👂 Auditory learners benefit from talking about as many words that start with each letter as she thinks of. Ask your child to name at least five words per letter.

TIME: 15 minutes

MATERIALS

- nontoxic glue
- paper
- markers
- art supplies (glitter, sequins, beads, pipe cleaners, colored rice, and glue)

Mastery occurs when: your child can name words that begin with each letter and can write each letter correctly on paper.

You may want to help your child a little more if: she can't name words that begin with each letter and can't write each letter correctly.

Mechanics of Writing

Learning to write letters, words, and sentences is hard for your kindergartner. Writing from left to right, staying within the lines on the paper, and correctly forming letters are a lot for a child to learn.

Gaining control of small motor skills is the first step to writing; the second step is to direct the small movements as actions that produce marks on paper in specific ways. The first thing you do is show your child how to form the letters. This is surprisingly simple but is often overlooked in lieu of simply writing the letter down and telling a child to "copy it." Start by writing the letter while your child is watching; describe the process while you do so. For example, if you're writing a lowercase "b," you would say "Draw a line straight down and then trace your pencil back up the same line to the middle. Now draw half a circle down the right side and close it at the bottom of the line." Say the same thing while your child tries writing the letter on his or her own. Feel free to start out by using dotted-line letters for your child to trace while he or she becomes familiar with the shape of new letters.

Writing letters leads to writing words, which finally leads to writing full sentences. You can make that leap a little easier by talking about how you are writing when you write. It is like "thinking aloud" about the mechanics of writing as you write. For example, begin writing a sentence while saying, "Sentences begin with capital letters, so I'll put one here" or "This is a complete sentence, so I'll put a period at the end," and so on.

In the beginning stages, your child's writing may not look a lot like the writing you want to see, but that is okay. Beginning writers easily disregard the lines on the paper, forget about writing from left to right, and have trouble keeping pencils steady. Rest assured that these things are normal and, with practice and gentle correction, will be overcome.

Taking writing from lines on a paper to a written message with meaning is a big part of kindergarten writing. Because your child is also learning to read letters on the basis of how they look and sound, your child's first written messages will be based on the sounds he or she

Mechanics of Writing Skills	Having Problems?	Quick Tips
Writes using sight words and sound spelling	Continually asks me to write for her	Be patient and write as your child dictates words to you. This is a basic step in the process of learning to write independently. You may want to try reading it together after you have written it, or ask your child to illustrate the writing. Young children like to read and reread stories.
Writes words and sentences from the left to right	Doesn't seem interested in writing	Provide activities that involve using eye-hand coordination in the same ways that writing does. Some examples are using stamps and stamp pads, tempera paint with a 1-inch paintbrush, lacing cards, magnetic letters, colored sidewalk chalk, washable markers, etc.
Writes all the letters of the alphabet and numbers from 1 to 10 correctly	Writes some numbers and letters backwards	This is perfectly normal for a child under the age of eight; it does not mean that your child has a learning problem. This child needs more experience seeing the letters and numbers as well as writing them. Playing bingo with your child is an excellent activity.

hears in the words. For example, "I no th wa" means "I know the way" to your child. Writing words the way he hears them is a good sign, and it is normal. The significance of this stage in your child's development is that he or she knows that writing means something, and he or she knows that written words are represented by the sounds in them. "Silent letters" are confusing, and your child isn't ready to focus on them. You can mention them and talk about them in context, but don't make a point of them yet.

Writing Activities

1 Sound Spelling

TIME: 10–15 minutes

MATERIALS
- paper
- pencil or marker
- list of three-letter words with the same vowel in the middle, such as "hat," "pal," "cat," and "can"

Learning happens when: you demonstrate "thinking aloud" in this activity. Say the word, write the word, and then blend the sounds to read it to your child. Next, say a word and ask your child to spell it on the paper. Do this for five words. You can repeat the activity with another set of five words with a different vowel sound.

Variations: Use the same activity, except use four-letter words that begin with two consonants beside each other whose sounds blend together. Examples are "st," "th," "ch," "gl," "sw," and "dr." These are called blends. This is another activity that can be repeated periodically until your child has mastered this skill.

👁 Visual learners may better succeed at this activity if you write the vowel sound on a paper in front of him or at the top of the paper he is writing on. Let your visual learner write the word as he is saying it.

 Kinesthetic learners can have trouble with beginning writing because they have to sit still and concentrate on very small movements. Let your child write the words outside with side-walk chalk, "write" with his finger in a box of sand, or spray shaving cream to form the letter on the wall by the bathtub.

🦻 Auditory learners will naturally say the word after you and make the sounds of each letter as they write it. Let your child talk while he writes; make sure that you say and sound each word slowly. Ask your child to name a few extra words with the same sounds.

Mastery occurs when: your child can correctly spell five three-letter words.

You may want to help your child a little more if: he can't correctly spell the three-letter words.

2 Apostrophe What?

Before you begin, spend some time discussing memories of the day the photos were taken. Then explain that you'll be writing down your child's story about the photographs.

TIME: 20 minutes

MATERIALS
▪ paper
▪ pencil or marker
▪ 3–4 photographs of your family taken at the same event or family activity

Learning happens when: your child dictates three to four complete sentences to you about the event in the photographs. Demonstrate "thinking aloud" concerning capitalization, punctuation, and spacing between words as you write. Reread the story to your child and call attention to the fact that all the sentences stick to the same subject. Help your child check that all the sentences are complete and not fragments by rereading the story, emphasizing punctuation by changing the pitch of your voice.

Variations: Follow the same directions, but purposely include some mistakes in the sentence writing. Lead your child to discover the mistakes and orally correct them.

👁 Visual learners pay close attention to what you are writing. Ask your child to pick a word or words that she would like to learn to spell; write those on paper so that your child can copy the spelling underneath your writing.

✋ Kinesthetic learners can act out the story after you finish writing it.

👂 Ask your auditory learner to reread the story out loud with you. Keep in mind that your child may be "reading" what he hears—in other words, repeating back to you what he remembers.

Mastery occurs when: your child can dictate a complete sentence that matches the pictures.

You may want to help your child a little more if: she can't dictate a complete sentence.

3 How Was Your Day?

TIME: 20 minutes

MATERIALS
- paper
- pencil or marker

On a sheet of paper, write a few sentence frames. Base the number of sentence frames on your child's readiness for writing. For example, "Today I _____." Talk about the day with your child; ask some specific questions and list words or phrases on your paper. Then ask your child to complete the sentence frames you have prepared. Your child will really like that this activity is about something personal to him.

Learning happens when: your child fills in the blanks with words that make sense and reads the sentences to you.

Variations: Use the same procedure for planning the day, the weekend, or another specific event that is yet to come.

👁 Visual learners should be encouraged to draw a picture to illustrate each sentence. Your child will enjoy using colored markers when completing the sentence frames.

✋ Follow the described procedure, but try letter stamps and a stamp pad for your kinesthetic learner to use for spelling.

👂 Auditory learners can extend the activity orally by telling you more details about his day.

Mastery occurs when: your child can fill in the blanks with correctly spelled words and phrases.

You may want to help your child a little more if: he can't fill in the blanks with correctly spelled words and phrases.

 **Verb Pictures**

Before beginning the activity, explain to your child that verbs are words that describe action.

Learning happens when: your child looks through the magazines, coloring books, and catalogues, cuts out five pictures depicting actions, and glues them to the paper. She should then name the action while you write the word under the picture. Reread each word as you point to the corresponding picture. Prepare an appropriate sentence frame for each action and have your child complete it by searching the page for the appropriate word and writing it down.

Variations: Use the same technique, but cut out pictures of nouns.

TIME: 20–25 minutes

MATERIALS
- scissors
- glue
- paper
- pencil
- old magazines, coloring books, or catalogues

👁 Visual learners are good at looking for the pictures, so ask her to find more pictures each time you do this activity. Create a word poster using the verbs. Keep this poster so that your child can refer to it for spelling later. It should also be used as a sight word list to read and review periodically.

✋ Kinesthetic learners can pantomime a verb while you try to guess what it is. Say the word slowly and ask your child to tell you the letters that make the sounds as you write them. Create a word poster using the verbs; keep this poster so that your child can refer to it for spelling later. It should also be used as a sight word list to read and review periodically.

👂 Your auditory learner will learn more from this activity if you allow her to talk about the pictures. Write the word she tells you about the picture and then let her tell you what else she sees in the picture. If she is interested, let your child dictate a sentence for you to write and then practice reading together.

Mastery occurs when: your child can identify the names of the actions in five pictures and then correctly finish the sentence frames with the appropriate actions.

You may want to help your child a little more if: she can't identify the correct actions to finish the sentences. You may want to limit the picture choices to make the activity a little easier. As your child improves this skill, you can add more choices.

5 Creative Writing

TIME: 20 minutes

MATERIALS
- book about feelings, such as *Rainbow Fish* or *Alexander and the Terrible, Horrible, No Good, Very Bad Day*
- markers
- paper
- pencil

Learning happens when: your child identifies feelings from the book and writes three or four sentences about what makes him happy. Talk about what punctuation to use for the sentences. Ask your child questions, such as "What punctuation mark sounds like a smile when you say the sentence? Yes, it's an exclamation point." "How do you make an exclamation point?" "Would you put an exclamation point after this sentence?"

Variations: Use different books as springboards for writing.

- Visual learners enjoy looking at the pictures in the book, so ask your child to draw a rainbow fish or perhaps another "rainbow" animal using colored paper and markers.

- Ask your kinesthetic learner to follow directions to make his own rainbow fish and write a sentence about it. You can find a fish pattern at www.knowledgeessentials.com.

- Ask your auditory learner to listen closely to the story and talk about his feelings. You could sing songs about feelings, such as "It Ain't Easy Being Green," by Kermit the Frog, "Shake Your Sillies Out," or "If You're Happy and You Know It."

Mastery occurs when: your child can identify several feelings from the book and can write about a time he felt happy or felt one of the other feelings in the book.

You may want to help your child a little more if: he can't correctly identify the character's feelings in the book(s). Try asking him questions about what happens to the character.

Grammar

Grammar is another element of kindergarten writing. Kindergarten grammar instruction is very basic and builds on the knowledge of how letters make up words and words make up sentences. Kindergartners are introduced to punctuation at the end of sentences and to capitalization of names, the pronoun "I," and the first word of a sentence. Verb tense and the correct use of pronouns are also introduced.

Grammar Skills	Having Problems?	Quick Tips
Puts a punctuation mark at the end of a sentence	Puts periods at the end of the line instead of at the end of a sentence	Orally practice recognizing sentences and sentence fragments. When you read a sentence out loud, emphasize the end of a sentence by changing the pitch in your voice; indicate a period with a pause. Explain that sentences tell whole thoughts. Use facial expressions as you read sentences and let your child decide if the sentence asks a question, tells you something, or shows excitement, and then talk about the correct punctuation for that expression.
Writes name beginning with a capital letter	Doesn't know where to use capital letters when writing	Sometimes children do this when they don't remember the way to make the capital letters. Check to see if this is the case. If so, then review letter matching and handwriting. Play memory games matching capital and lowercase letters.
Uses letters to write words	Writes illegibly Misspells words	These difficulties are perfectly normal. A child just learning to spell words will usually leave out silent letters and disregard the v-c-v pattern for spelling long vowel sounds. Ask your child to read her writing to you. If she can't read it, then you need to talk about spelling again.

Grammar Activities

 Is This a Sentence?

Learning happens when: your child plays a sentence game with you. Define a sentence to your child as a group of words that express a complete thought. Say a word, phrase, or sentence, then ask your child to repeat it and tell you whether it is a sentence. (For example, "No, thank you, I don't want to go.") Keep them simple.

TIME: 15 minutes

Variations: Say a phrase or word and challenge your child to use it in a complete sentence.

- 👁 Visual learners may prefer to look for pictures in a magazine and then tell you a sentence that describes the picture. Make sure your child tells you a complete sentence. If you prefer, ask your child to write a sentence for the picture.

- ✋ Ask your kinesthetic learner to perform an action (such as to pick up the crayons), and as soon as he finishes that action ask him to tell you a sentence about what he just did. Make sure your child tells you a complete sentence.

- 👂 Ask your auditory learner to recite a chant or rhyme with you (for example, "Peanut Butter," "Five Green and Speckled Frogs," or "There Was an Old Woman Who Swallowed a Fly"). Afterwards, ask your child to tell you a complete sentence from the chant or rhyme.

Mastery occurs when: your child can recognize a complete sentence.

You may want to help your child a little more if: she is unable to write or tell a complete sentence. Try reading a favorite book with your child and asking your child to follow the sentences you are reading with her finger.

2 | Can You Find a Sentence?

TIME: 20 minutes

MATERIALS
■ storybook

Learning happens when: you ask your child to tell you what she knows about sentences. This will be your guide as to where to start instruction. Some children will know that a sentence starts with a capital letter and ends with punctuation; others will not. Read the story to your child. Ask her to point to a sentence in the book and explain how she knows that the sentence begins there. Do the same with the end of the sentence.

Variations: Instead of following the entire sentence with a finger, ask your child to point to the beginning and end of each sentence as you are reading it.

👁 Ask your visual learner to sit next to you while you read and watch you track the words with your finger. At the end of each page, ask your child to show you where a sentence starts and stops.

✋ Ask your kinesthetic learner to sit next to you while you read and watch you track the words with your finger. At the end of each page, ask your child to draw the letter that a sentence starts with and the punctuation at the end of the sentence. Then you find and read the sentence on the page.

👂 Ask your auditory learner to sit next to you while you read and track the words with your finger. Ask your child to tell you a sentence from the page you just read and together find the beginning and end of the sentence. Talk about the way to recognize them.

Mastery occurs when: your child can look at a page in an age-appropriate book and show you a sentence.

You may want to help your child a little more if: she is unable to follow the sentence. Try asking your child to trace the outside of the beginning word of the sentence with her finger. Talk about how the first word in a sentence looks different from the other words.

3 Capitalization

Learning happens when: you explain that capital letters are used when writing a person's name, a proper noun, or the pronoun "I." Say a noun; let your child tell you whether it should have a capital letter or not and talk about why it would need a capital letter. Then write the word for your child.

TIME: 15 minutes

MATERIALS
- paper
- marker or pencil

Variations: Read a book to your child and point out the words that are capitalized. If he can, have your child explain why the words have capital letters. If your child can't do this yet, explain the reason to him.

- 👁 Have your visual learner sit with you as you read a book to him. Point out the words that begin with capital letters and ask your child to explain why they are capitalized.

- ✋ Ask your kinesthetic learner to copy the word that you wrote (using the space that you left near the word), then tell you the reason for the capital letter.

- 👂 Ask your auditory learner to do the variation of this activity; because it involves more talking, he will relate better to this activity.

Mastery occurs when: your child can tell you why words have capital letters.

4 Punctuation

TIME: 15 minutes

MATERIALS
- paper
- marker or pen

Learning happens when: you talk with your child about the kinds of sentences that use periods, exclamation marks, and question marks. Give her examples by using voice inflections to stress the differences. Show her the punctuation marks used with each of the sentences and name the marks. Play a game in which you say a sentence and your child names the punctuation mark that should be at the end of that sentence. Then ask your child to switch roles with you. Take turns doing this until your child gets bored.

- 👁 Visual learners should practice making the punctuation marks. Have your child use colored markers and make artistic designs when making the period, exclamation point, and question mark.

- ✋ Perform a finger play for your kinesthetic learner. Exaggerate the expression in your voice and actions, and pause at the end of a sentence to allow your child to name the punctuation mark.

- 👂 Ask your auditory learner to read along with you as you use expression to read a patterned, predictable book. Talk about the different punctuation marks in the book.

Mastery occurs when: your child can identify and name a period, question mark, and exclamation point. She can match the way a sentence sounds to the type of punctuation that should be used.

5 | Word Building

Write a consonant on each side of the cube with the marker (cube 1: "b," "f," "k," "h," "p," "m"; cube 2: "d," "n," "r," "s," "t," "l"). Use only one cube at a time. On the paper write "_at."

TIME: 15 minutes

MATERIALS
- 2 cubes
- marker
- paper

Learning happens when: your child creates words by rolling the cube (die) to find the beginning sound of the word. Ask your child to write the beginning sound on the blank line, blend the sounds, and read the word. Continue until the words begin to repeat themselves, then change die if your child is still interested in the game.

Variations: Follow the procedure described, but instead of using a cube, have your child draw letters from a gift bag (or paper bag) for the first letter of the word.

- 👁 Visual learners will do this activity with very little assistance and can write the list of words themselves, after you model writing the ending. They could draw pictures to illustrate the meaning of the words they write.

- ✋ Ask your kinesthetic learner to follow the described procedure to form words, but use an ordinary numbered die and an alphabet line (similar to a number line). Your child rolls the die to determine the number of spaces to count on the alphabet line in order to find the beginning letter.

- 👂 Ask your auditory learner to explain the game to an older sibling or adult family member. That person would then follow his directions to play for a while.

Mastery occurs when: your child can change the beginning sound of a word and then read the new word, after you model the activity.

You may want to help your child a little more if: he has trouble writing a word from the letters he rolls. Try brainstorming words that end with the sounds you are working on (such as "at"). Say the words out loud, then ask your child to roll the die and complete the activity as described above.

Environmental Learning

Five-year-old children are naturally self-centered. Therefore, the most interesting words to a five-year-old are ones that have personal meaning to her, such as her first name or her age. Take advantage of this at every opportunity and encourage your child to remember words in her environment. The name on your mailbox; signs on your street; public restroom signs; enter, exit, on, and off signs; and names of family members are all good examples. Make lists of these words and place them in visible areas for your child (use magnets to place lists at eye level on the refrigerator). Periodically have your child copy the words on paper or say the words out loud.

End of Kindergarten Writing Checklist

Students who are working at the standard level at the end of kindergarten:

____ Form letters

____ Correspond sounds with writing

____ Name and label objects

____ Maintain focus

____ Gather, collect, and share information

____ Incorporate storybook language (for example, "Once upon a time") into their writing

____ Write in chronological order

Kindergarten Math

7

It's hard to believe that your baby is growing up and doing mathematics! Math is a big part of your child's day. Although math may cause some of you to relive painful memories of endless worksheets, math should be painless and can even be fun in kindergarten. Your child will be exploring, experimenting, counting, sorting, and explaining.

Young children often have trouble with symbolic concepts. For this reason, the early childhood classroom uses *manipulatives*. A manipulative is anything that your child can count or handle that helps him or her learn a concept. Typical math manipulatives found in the classroom include cubes, dice, pattern blocks, clocks, and puzzles. For example, when someone says "three," adults have no trouble visualizing three objects and the numeral 3, but it's not as simple for children. By having

---

Beginning of Kindergarten Math Checklist

Students who are working at the standard level at the beginning of kindergarten:

—— Count to ten

—— Count a set of five objects using one-to-one correspondence

—— Identify the numerals 1–5

—— Compare sets of objects and describe them using "more," "less," "equal," or "same"

—— Use correct vocabulary to compare objects ("big," "small"; "long," "short"; "more," "less;" "heavy," "light")

—— Use words that identify time of day ("morning," "afternoon," "night," "day")

—— Identify circles, squares, rectangles, and triangles when shown models

—— Sort objects by their attributes (color, size, shape, and so on)

—— Use words that indicate position ("in," "out," "beside," "over," "under," "between")

—— Recognize and copy patterns in songs, rhymes, and body movements

something concrete like a manipulative to work with, children eventually bridge the gap between the physical world and the world of symbols and abstract concepts. For example, a child learning basic addition facts may start by using manipulatives to help him or her solve the problem. If the problem is 5 + 3, your child may make one group of five cubes and one group of three cubes. To find the sum, he or she will then put the groups together and count the total. By using manipulatives, your child will understand that addition is putting groups together. The cubes serve as a bridge to the symbolic 5 + 3 = 8.

Your child will be doing math in three general settings. The first is the large group setting. Most math concepts will be taught in a large group setting through calendar activities, direct lessons, everyday routines, graphing, sorting, and counting rhymes. Kindergarten classes begin with the calendar activities of recalling the day of the week and the month, locating the day on the calendar, reciting the date, adding a number to a running list of the days of school, and reading the numbers chorally. There's also usually a graphing activity involving the daily weather. The second setting is in centers. A center is a place in the room where children can independently practice a concept. For example, your child may visit the math center and practice counting items. The center will change regularly as new concepts are introduced. The third setting is either small group or one-on-one instruction with the teacher. The teacher may use this setting to help struggling students or to challenge children who need more rigorous instruction.

The typical kindergarten math program will have two major components. The first is developing number sense and exploring patterns. The second is studying geometry and measurement.

Number Sense and Patterns

Number sense is very important for success in mathematics. It is a set of math skills that describes your child's understanding that numbers

Number Sense and Pattern Skills	Having Problems?	Quick Tips
Tells whether one set has more, less, or the same number of items as another set	Is unable to tell whether a set has more, less, or the same number of items as another set	Practice counting two sets to determine whether one set has more, less, or the same number of items. Many kindergartners cannot tell by only looking, or they may erroneously say one set has more simply because the items that make up the set are physically larger than the items in the other set. Ask your child to look in the flatware drawer and tell you if there are more spoons or forks in the drawer. Provide multiple opportunities to compare sets using various manipulatives.
Pairs and counts items using one-to-one correspondence	Cannot pair and count items	Ask your child to help set the table. By placing a napkin and fork at each place setting, he is practicing one-to-one correspondence.
Counts forward to twenty and backward from ten	Has difficulty counting forward to twenty and backward from ten	This is where those counting songs are helpful. You can sing counting songs with your child; there are also many high-quality early childhood music CDs that have counting songs on them. Children often learn concepts more easily with music.
Counts up to ten objects	Has trouble counting objects	Counting objects is different from just rote counting, because it requires an understanding of one-to-one correspondence. Ask your child to count at every opportunity. Ask her to count how many eggs are left in the carton, how many pens are in the pen holder, how many cans of soda are left in the refrigerator, and so on.
Writes the numerals 0 through 10	Has difficulty writing the numerals	Writing numerals requires practice. Do not worry if your child reverses some of the numerals. As is true with letter reversal, this is very common at this age. Give your child lots of opportunities to read the numerals so that he will internalize the shape of them. Ask your child to practice writing numerals that have relevance, such as his age, telephone number, and so on.
Sorts or groups different objects into sets that have similar characteristics	Cannot group like items in a set	Start by asking your child to sort by color—for example, using a handful of different-colored beads. Once she can sort by color, ask her to sort a group by a different characteristic, such as sorting shoes into one group that has laces and another group that does not have laces.

Number Sense and Pattern Skills	Having Problems?	Quick Tips
Explains and extends simple patterns	Has trouble explaining and extending patterns	Color patterns are probably the easiest to start with. Get some M&Ms. Pick two colors and make a simple pattern, such as yellow-orange-yellow-orange-yellow. Ask your child to verbalize the color pattern and to tell what color comes next. Continue with different colors and patterns.

represent quantity and that you can use numbers to count quantity, or "how many." Children who develop number sense understand the order in math. They see the relationships that numbers have to one another; they understand how numbers are put together and taken apart; and they have an intuitive sense about our number system. The kindergarten classroom develops number sense through counting activities, working with sets of objects, pairing items together, and comparing quantities in groups.

Working with patterns is another very important concept in mathematics. In kindergarten, your child will be working with patterns by sorting and grouping objects into sets and by explaining and extending simple patterns. Learning to recognize and extend patterns is a skill that will have many applications beyond the mathematics classroom. The ability to recognize patterns will help your child in language arts, social studies, science, and games and sports. This skill is a powerful one to develop.

Number Sense and Patterns Activities

1 Snack Counting

Learning happens when: your child counts the number of cookies in the package. Help your child open the cookies and pour them on a plate. Ask your child to count the number of cookies that were in the bag.

TIME: 15 minutes

MATERIALS
- paper plate
- individual package of mini-cookies

Variations: Do the same activity, but add the element of writing down the number of cookies on a sheet of paper. Tracing or copying is okay, if necessary.

👁 Visual learners will benefit from seeing the number represented visually with objects (for example, "So twelve cookies look like this!"). Use the variation for your child.

✋ Kinesthetic learners enjoy opening the package and moving the cookies as they count. Ask your child to open another package and compare the quantities in the two packages to see if they are exactly the same, using one-to-one correspondence. If they are not, explain that another way that quantity is measured is by weight.

👂 Auditory learners will count the cookies aloud. They can eat the cookies as you read a book about cookies (such as *If You Give a Mouse a Cookie*, by Laura Joffe Numeroff).

Mastery occurs when: your child can successfully count the number of cookies in an individual bag.

You may want to help your child a little more if: he is having difficulty counting the cookies. Sometimes young children will try to count items randomly, and they will lose track of which items have been counted and which have not. If this is the case with your child, prepare two small plates. Put all the cookies on the first plate. As your child counts a cookie, have him move it to the other plate. Continue counting cookies in this manner until all the cookies are on the second plate. If your child still has trouble, count along with him, showing how you count items in a very orderly manner. You will be modeling how to do it, and eventually your child will be able to do it on his own.

2 | Number Hopscotch

TIME: 15 minutes

MATERIALS
- die
- sidewalk chalk

Learning happens when: you draw a hopscotch on the sidewalk outside your house. Explain that you and your child are going to play the game using a die to indicate the number of hops. Take turns with your child rolling the die, counting the dots on the die, and hopping the number of times indicated by the die. The game requires recognizing numbers and using one-to-one correspondence in moving on the hopscotch. Play until your child tires of the game.

Variations: Use any game that involves counting. Playing board games, dominoes, or cards can reinforce various math skills.

- 👁 Visual learners will be able to see quickly how to make the correct moves and move the correct number without counting out loud. Show her how to make tally marks to keep score.
- ✋ This is a great activity for your kinesthetic learner. She will benefit from the movement of the game and tossing the die.
- 👂 Auditory learners can count the correct number of spaces to move for each roll of the die for both players.

Mastery occurs when: your child can read the die and hop the correct number of spaces on the hopscotch.

You may want to help your child a little more if: she is having trouble hopping the correct number of spaces. Count along with your child to help strengthen her counting skills. After some practice and modeling, your child will be able to do this independently.

3 Counting Cards

Prepare the deck of cards by removing the face cards. Shuffle the deck and place it facedown.

Time: 10 minutes

Materials
■ deck of cards

Learning happens when: your child counts the number of items on a card and makes the connection between the number of items and the numeral. Ask your child to draw one card and count the number of spades, hearts, clubs, or diamonds in its center. Continue in the same manner for the rest of the deck. Although this activity may seem simple, some children need practice counting, and counting shapes on the cards requires children to count objects and match them to a written number.

Once your child can easily count the shapes on the card, play a modified game of War. Place two cards at a time on the table and ask your child to slap the card with the higher number. Let your child pick up the card with the higher number and make a stack. When your child has ten cards, he has won. This game can be played with one or more players.

Variations: Prepare a deck of cards as previously instructed. Give your child a piece of paper and a pencil. Show him a card, covering the numerals in opposite corners. Ask him to count the items and write the numeral on the paper. Continue in the same way with the other cards.

👁 Visual learners typically make a quick connection between the picture of a number (the number of items on the card) and the numeral. Play a game of Go Fish using the cards.

🖐 Kinesthetic learners can sort the cards according to the numbers on the cards or according to suits (spades, clubs, diamonds, hearts); he can talk with you about his observations while he is sorting.

👂 Auditory learners will count aloud and talk about the activity. They can sing a counting song or perform a counting finger play (for example, the song "Five Little Ducks Went Out One Day").

Mastery occurs when: your child can accurately count the shapes on each card and connect that number to the numeral.

You may want to help your child a little more if: he is having trouble counting accurately. Start with half the deck, using the cards with small numerals (ace to five). Once your child can accurately count to five, slowly add the larger cards.

4 | The Number Game

TIME: 10 minutes

MATERIALS
- large sheet of paper
- pen
- 2 dice
- 22 game pieces

The game pieces can be anything that will fit in the boxes that you will be drawing on the paper. For example, you may want to use poker chips, dried macaroni, or "o"-shaped cereal. Use the paper to make two game boards. Cut the paper in half lengthwise. On each half of the paper, draw eleven boxes in a row, large enough to go across the length of the page and large enough so a number can be written inside. Write the numbers 2 through 12 in the boxes, one number per box. The two game boards should be identical. Each board will look something like the figure here.

2	3	4	5	6	7	8	9	10	11	12

Learning happens when: you and your child play a game that requires counting, adding, and recognizing numerals. Both you and your child will get a game board and eleven game pieces. First, both of you will roll a die. The person who rolls the largest number goes first. The first player takes the two dice and rolls them. He or she will count the total number of dots on both dice. Player one will cover that number on the game board with one of the game pieces. Play then goes to player two. Player two will continue in the same way. If a player rolls a number that is already covered, no action can be taken, and play goes to the other player. The winner is the first player to cover all eleven numbered spaces on the game board.

Variations: Make a similar game board with seventeen boxes. Number the boxes 2 through 18. Play a variation of the same game with three dice and thirty-six game pieces.

👁 Visual learners make a quick connection between the number of dots and the numeral that goes with that number. Extend this activity by having your child graph the number of times each numeral on the die is rolled. You will need a graph containing six lines with six to ten boxes in each. Each time your child tosses the die, she should mark an X in a box. The first line to be filled wins the game.

✌ Kinesthetic learners like the physical aspect of rolling the dice and covering the numbers. This child may want to play another game and help put away the game pieces when finished.

🦻 Auditory learners can describe the activity to the family at dinnertime using the game board as a prop.

Mastery occurs when: your child can accurately count the dots and connect the number of dots to the numeral on the game board.

You may want to help your child a little more if: she is having trouble counting the dots. If necessary, make a game board with six squares, numbered 1 through 6. Play the game with one die. Once your child is successful with one die, play the version with two dice.

5 Cookie Math

TIME: 15 minutes

MATERIALS
■ package of various-shaped cookies (animals or shapes)
■ 12 × 18-inch sheet of construction paper

Prepare a graph by folding the construction paper lengthwise into fourths. This paper is the format for your child's graph.

Learning happens when: your child makes a graph of the different shapes of cookies and analyzes the results. Ask your child to open the cookies and sort the shapes. Ask him to line them up in each section of the graph. Next ask him to count the number of cookies in each section. Finally, ask him questions about the cookies, such as which shape has the most cookies and which shape has the fewest.

Variations: This activity can be adapted to use different objects; your child can sort candy by color, animal crackers by animal, a mix of dried beans by type of bean, and so on.

👁 Visual learners can draw pictures of the cookies and write the total of each shape under the picture.

 Kinesthetic learners can compare the cookie shapes using one-to-one correspondence.

🜋 Auditory learners can describe how they sorted the cookies. They should then compare the lines of the graph orally using "more than," "fewer than," and "same."

Mastery occurs when: your child can easily create the graph and compare the number of items in each category.

You may want to help your child a little more if: he is struggling with the task. Be very sequential, asking your child to complete one step before moving on to the next. You may need to model how to do it by doing the first few steps with him. If your child is struggling with comparing the number of cookies in each row, make sure the cookies in each category are directly lined up above and below one another. Then ask your child which cookie makes the longest train. The cookies must be lined up carefully so that your child is not fooled by larger cookies making a longer train.

6 Goldfish Addition

Learning occurs when: your child uses the goldfish crackers to solve addition and subtraction problems. Tell your child that you are going to tell her some stories about the goldfish. As you tell the story, ask your child to show the story on the paper towel, using the crackers. The following are some examples of stories you can tell:

TIME: 15 minutes

MATERIALS
▪ goldfish crackers
▪ paper towel

- Four goldfish were playing around the coral reef. (Ask your child to put the number of goldfish playing on the paper towel.) Two goldfish had to go home. (Ask your child to show two goldfish going home.) How many goldfish are left?

- Six goldfish were on the school bus. Three more goldfish got on the bus. How many are on the bus now?

- Five goldfish were playing hopscotch. One decided to play something else and left. How many goldfish are playing hopscotch now?

- Two goldfish were playing at home. Three more came over. How many are playing now?

Feel free to make up your own stories. Your child will love it if you add elements to the story that reflect her interests and use her name, if possible. For example, if your child loves art, you could make up a story involving art, such as "Tara was painting a picture of the sea. She painted three goldfish on her picture. Tara decided the picture needed more goldfish, so she painted three more goldfish. How many fish are on Tara's picture?"

Variations: Once your child can easily perform this task, add the writing element. Show your child how the story can be written in number form. Ask her to write the math problem that goes with the story. You may need to do this with her several times, until she makes the connection between the words in the story and numbers and operations, and can do it independently. If writing is a problem, use index cards to make a set of numbers 0 to 9 and an addition, subtraction, and equal sign. Your child then uses the index cards to show the math problem.

- 👁 Visual learners enjoy seeing the visual representation of the problem and should be asked to write the number sentence.

- ✋ Kinesthetic learners represent the math problem by "building the problem," combining the groups to find the total or separating the group to find the difference. Ask your child to show you the number sentence using the index cards in the variation.

- 👂 Auditory learners listen to the story and orally count each group of fish. Ask your child to say the number sentence that is in each story.

Mastery occurs when: your child can easily use the crackers to show what is happening in a story problem.

You may want to help your child a little more if: she is having trouble determining what to do with the crackers. There are three basic parts to a story problem: setup, action, and conclusion. Ask your child clarifying questions at each part. For example, the story setup may be "There were seven goldfish at a birthday party." Ask your child these questions: (1) "How many goldfish were at the party?" (2) "So how many goldfish should you put on your paper towel?" (3) "Show me on the paper towel." The action part of the problem may be "Three more goldfish arrive." Ask your child these questions: (1) "How many goldfish arrived?" (2) "Does that mean more fish are coming to the party or that fish are leaving the party?" (3) "Show me what it looks like when three more fish come to the party." The conclusion will be the question, "How many goldfish are at the party now?" Ask your child what needs to be done to tell how many goldfish are at the party now. Then ask your child to count the total number of goldfish on the towel.

7 | Spill the Beans

Prepare the beans by asking your child to use the permanent marker to color one side of each lima bean. (If this might be too messy, please feel free to do it yourself. Alternatively, you can go outside, lay the lima beans on a piece of newspaper, and spray-paint the beans on one side only. When they dry, you will have two-color beans.)

Learning happens when: your child uses the lima beans to create and write addition sentences. Put the ten beans in the paper cup. Ask your child to shake and spill the beans. Some of the beans

TIME: 15 minutes

MATERIALS
- 10 dried lima beans
- small paper cup
- colored permanent marker
- paper
- pencil

will land color side up; others will land white side up. Ask your child these three questions: (1) "How many beans are white?" (2) "How many beans are red [or whatever color you used]?" (3) "How many beans are there in all?" Finally, ask your child to write this as an addition problem. For example, if there were six white beans and four red beans, your child would write 6 + 4 = 10 or 4 + 6 = 10. You may have to model this for him several times before he will be able to do it independently. Repeat this several more times.

Variations: Write and solve a subtraction sentence. Start by having your child shake and spill the beans. Ask him to count the total number of beans that were spilled. Then ask him to take away the white beans. Now how many beans are there? Finally, have your child write this as a subtraction sentence. Each subtraction sentence should start with "10 −," because there is a total of ten beans.

- 👁 Visual learners will enjoy the visual pattern of the beans when they are spilled. They will probably make a quick connection between the manipulatives (the spilled beans) and the symbolic math sentence.

- ✋ Kinesthetic learners will enjoy gathering the beans, shaking the cup, spilling the beans, and writing the number sentence.

- 👂 Auditory learners will enjoy the sounds of shaking and spilling the beans and orally counting the beans and telling you the number sentence.

Please note: This was adapted from a *Math Their Way* activity written by Mary Baratta-Lorton (Reading, MA: Addison-Wesley, 1974).

8 Money Patterns

Learning happens when: your child uses the coins to identify and extend different patterns. Lay the coins in a simple AB pattern. (An AB pattern alternates elements, so the pattern would be penny, nickel, penny, nickel, penny, nickel.) Ask your child to say the pattern aloud, using the correct name for the coins. Then ask her to add coins to keep the pattern going. Lay a new pattern, such as an ABB pattern (penny, nickel, nickel, penny, nickel, nickel). Ask your child to say the pattern aloud and extend the pattern with the other coins. Continue in the same way. Other possible patterns include, for example, AAB (penny, penny, nickel) and AABB (penny, penny, nickel, nickel).

Variations: To extend the activity, after your child has identified and extended a pattern with the coins, give her ten beads of one color and ten beads of a different color and ask her to make the same pattern with the beads. For example, if your child just completed the AB pattern with coins, she will lay out the beads in an AB pattern.

- 👁 Visual learners can easily observe the similarities and differences in the coins. Give your child paper and crayons so she can draw the coins or make coin rubbings.

- ✍ Kinesthetic learners enjoy building the patterns. Ask your child to build her own patterns. Afterwards, ask her to make stacks of each type of coin.

- 👂 Ask your auditory learner to read the pattern out loud.

Mastery occurs when: your child can identify and extend the patterns.

TIME: 15 minutes

MATERIALS
- 10 pennies
- 10 nickels

You may want to help your child a little more if: she is having trouble identifying the patterns. Ask your child to verbalize the pattern out loud. Verbalizing a pattern while looking at it can help some children identify the pattern. Once your child can verbalize the pattern, ask her to continue verbalizing it while she lays down the appropriate coins to extend it.

9 Colorful Candy Patterns

TIME: 15 minutes

MATERIALS
■ bag of different-colored candy (or button collection)
■ paper towel(s)

Learning happens when: your child uses candy to build color patterns across the paper towel. Ask your child to make four patterns with the candy. Then ask your child to read the patterns to you. There are many different colors, so your child can go beyond the AB patterns to ABC patterns, ABCD patterns, and so on.

Variations: Dictate the patterns to be built and read the pattern together.

👁 Visual learners can represent the patterns by drawing them using markers and paper; they may be able to label each of the patterns they draw.

✋ Kinesthetic learners should use the candies to build a pattern that is different from any that you built together, then name the pattern.

👂 Because auditory learners will enjoy talking about the patterns and listening to your pattern dictations, you may want to use the variation for this activity instead.

Mastery occurs when: your child can build and describe patterns.

You may want to help your child a little more if: he is having trouble building patterns. In this case, start a pattern and ask your child to read the pattern and extend it. You will be modeling how to build patterns.

10 Pattern Hunt

Learning happens when: you and your child search for patterns in the house. There are patterns everywhere: on fabric, clothing, artwork, tile work, dinner plates, and more. Go on a search with your child for patterns. When you and your child find something that has a pattern, discuss it together. Ask your child for her opinion about the pattern. You will probably be surprised at the patterns your child sees.

TIME: 10 minutes

Variations: If your child loves to draw, ask her to draw the patterns she finds.

- 👁 Visual learners can draw patterns from clothing (for example, a striped T-shirt).
- ✋ Kinesthetic learners will benefit from the physical activity of searching the house. Try introducing a stopwatch and see how many patterns your child can find in two minutes.
- 👂 Auditory learners may walk through the house with you and talk about the patterns she finds in different rooms.

Mastery occurs when: your child can locate patterns throughout the house.

You may want to help your child a little more if: she is having trouble finding patterns. Play a version of I Spy with patterns. When you spot a pattern, say, "I spy, with my eye, something that is . . ." Finish the sentence with a descriptive word about the pattern. Ask your child to find the pattern in the room.

Geometry and Measurement

Although most people think of geometry as some dreadful math class they had to take in high school, believe it or not your child will be studying two aspects of geometry in kindergarten. The first aspect deals with shapes. Kindergartners will learn to identify and draw basic shapes and shapes of everyday items in their environment. For example, a clock may have a circular face, or a window may be rectangular. Your child will learn the specific attributes that make up various shapes, and he or she will compare them—for example, noting that triangles having three sides whereas squares and rectangles have four sides. In addition to identifying, comparing, and drawing shapes, your child will be examining the results of combining different shapes.

The second aspect of geometry concerns spatial sense. Kindergartners will learn to accurately use words to describe the relative position and direction of two items. These descriptive words include "on," "above," "below," "beside," "under," "on top of," "behind," and "over."

Your child will also be studying measurement. Children usually start learning about measurement by using nonstandard units. For example, instead of using a ruler, a kindergartner may make a train of paper clips to measure the length of a pencil. Your child will also compare and order objects, such as putting pencils in order from shortest to longest or putting three balls in order from smallest to largest. Your child will begin looking at the tools used to measure. Kindergartners will learn that a ruler measures length, a scale measures weight, a clock and calendar measure time, and a thermometer measures temperature. Your child will identify the days of the week and months of the year, and he or she will begin reading a clock and telling time to the hour. Finally, your child will begin learning about currency by identifying pennies, nickels, dimes, and quarters.

Geometry and Measurement Skills	Having Problems?	Quick Tips
Identifies, compares, and draws basic shapes	Has difficulty identifying, comparing, or drawing shapes	Identify shapes with your child in your daily environment. Comment on them, so that she hears the name of the shape while looking at a physical representation of the shape. If your child needs more direct practice, make four flash cards. Draw each of the following shapes on the flash cards: circle, square, rectangle, and triangle. Make a game of seeing if your child can identify all four correctly. Talk about how a circle is different from the other three shapes because it is round. Talk about the number of sides the shapes have. Finally, talk about how a rectangle has four sides and a square is a special kind of rectangle with four equal sides.
Uses words such as "on," "above," "below," "beside," "under," "on top of," "behind," and "over" to describe position or direction	Confuses the terms	Ask your child to complete simple actions, such as putting a book "on" a table or sliding a box "under" the bed. Practice using these terms with your child. In addition, ask him to describe the position of objects by asking where something is.
Measures objects using nonstandard units	Has trouble measuring objects	Gather a group of items that can be used to measure, such as paper clips, clothespins, safety pins, or markers. Ask your child to measure an item by making a train of the measuring items next to the item being measured. Finally, have her count the train. For example, your child may use clothespins to measure a wooden spoon and find that the spoon is five clothespins long.
Compares and orders objects (e.g., long, longer, longest; small, medium, large, etc.)	Has trouble comparing objects	Gather several objects for your child to compare. Practice comparing them and putting them in order.
Identifies the tools used to measure length, weight, time, and temperature	Does not know what each tool measures	The best way for your child to understand this concept is through real-life application. Allow your child to help you measure things around the house. Post a thermometer outside a window and check the temperature with your child daily. Talk about items on the calendar, counting the days until a big event, or look at an hourly schedule of the day.

Geometry and Measurement Skills	Having Problems?	Quick Tips
Tells time to the nearest hour	Cannot tell time	Digital clocks are wonderful and are present everywhere. The problem is that many children are not exposed to analog clocks. Make sure there is at least one analog clock in your home. An analog clock that chimes on the hour would be ideal. Check the time on the analog clock with your child. Model how to tell time for him.
Identifies the days of the week and months of the year	Does not know the days of the week or months of the year	Talk about what day it is with your child. Extend this by talking about what day it was yesterday and what day it will be tomorrow. Also talk about the month. Using and looking at a large calendar posted in a common area will help your child learn the days of the week and months of the year.
Identifies pennies, nickels, dimes, and quarters	Has trouble identifying the different coins	If your child does not already have one, get her a piggy bank. Periodically empty the piggy bank and ask your child to divide the coins by putting all the pennies together, all the nickels together, and so on. By having her own money, your child will learn to identify the coins quickly.

Geometry and Measurement Activities

1   What's Your Position?

TIME: 15 minutes

MATERIALS

◼ triangle, square, rectangle, and circle cut out of poster board

◼ large sheet of construction paper

◼ 8 index cards

◼ marker

◼ *Apple Tree*, a rhyming story by Theo LeSieg (optional)

Prepare the index cards by writing one of the following words or phrases on each card: "above," "below," "beside," "next to," "under," "to the left of," "to the right of," and "on top of."

Learning happens when: your child follows your directions in placing the shapes onto the paper. *Apple Tree* is a good story to read with this activity, but it is not necessary for the completion of the activity. Mix the index cards and place them facedown in one pile. Have your child draw an index card and choose two shapes. Ask him to place one shape in relation to the other shape, as specified on the card. For example, if your child draws the "next to" card and a triangle and a circle card, he should put the triangle next to the circle. Once your child completes the task, have him draw another card, pick two shapes, and place the shapes as indicated by the card. Continue until all the cards are used. If you noticed that your child had difficulty with a particular word or phrase, practice using that term during the week.

Variations: Place two shapes on the paper and ask your child to describe the position of the shapes. If your child is having trouble identifying the word, let him pick the position as you read them from the index cards.

- Visual learners should connect the position word with "what it looks like." Ask her to place the index card in the spot that it represents (underneath the shapes, above the shapes, and so on).

- Kinesthetic learners can easily connect the word with a movement, so ask your kinesthetic learner to do what the index card says in the spot that it represents (stand beside the sofa, get underneath the table, and so on).

- Auditory learners should read the index cards out loud as they place the shapes and the card in the correct positions and then restate the sentence with the card in place ("The blue circle is above the red triangle").

Mastery occurs when: your child can place the shapes in the relative position as indicated by the card.

You may want to help your child a little more if: he struggles with the position words. Practice one position with several different shapes. (For example, have him put the circle to the right of the square, then put the rectangle to the right of the triangle, and finally put the triangle to the right of the circle.) Once your child can easily follow that direction, practice in the same way with a different position. Continue as needed.

2 Play Dough Shapes

TIME: 15 minutes

MATERIALS
- play dough
- rolling pin
- triangle-, star-, and circle-shaped cookie cutters

Learning happens when: your child makes shapes out of the play dough. Let your child have free play with the play dough for a few minutes. Next ask her to roll out the play dough with the rolling pin. Ask your child to use each cookie cutter to make the shapes. Once your child has finished making the shapes, ask her to identify them.

Variations: Instead of using the cookie cutters, ask your child to create the various shapes by hand using the play dough.

- 👁 Visual learners should be encouraged to decorate the shapes they make.

- ✋ Ask your kinesthetic learner to describe the feel of the play dough shapes. Ask her to try to make 3-D versions of the shapes (a ball for a circle, a box for a square, and so on).

- 👂 Encourage your auditory learner to talk about the process of making the shapes, the attributes of each shape, and their differences as she works.

Mastery occurs when: your child can create and identify the shapes.

You may want to help your child a little more if: she is having trouble making or identifying the shapes. Draw three to four on paper. Ask your child to make a rope with the play dough by rolling it out with her hands. She then uses the rope to go around the edge of each shape on the paper; ask your child to say the name of the shape as she is working.

3 | Coloring Book Shapes

TIME: 10 minutes

MATERIALS
- coloring book
- markers or crayons

Learning happens when: your child finds and colors shapes in the pictures of a coloring book. This activity is a little different from just coloring a picture, because your child needs to be selective about what he will color. Ask your child to select a picture that he likes in the coloring book. After he has chosen the picture, challenge him to find examples of circles, triangles, squares, and rectangles in the picture. Ask your child to color the shapes as he finds them.

Variations: Ask your child to color-code the shapes. For example, he could color all circles yellow, all squares green, all triangles orange, and all rectangles red.

- Visual learners can draw their own pictures using different shapes.
- Kinesthetic learners can keep a tally of the shapes on a separate sheet and count the tally marks when finished.
- Auditory learners can use their location words to describe the shapes in the pictures and their locations.

Mastery occurs when: your child can readily see the different shapes that compose a picture.

You may want to help your child a little more if: he is having trouble finding the shapes. Focus on one shape at a time and help your child locate that shape on the page. Once your child understands the task and is able to recognize each shape more easily, ask him to find the shapes in a different picture.

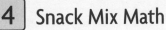 Snack Mix Math

MATERIALS
- cup of snack mix
- paper plate

Learning happens when: your child examines the snack mix and recognizes the different shapes. Pour the snack mix onto the paper plate. Ask your child to divide the snack mix into piles of circles, triangles, and so on. Once she has divided the snack mix, ask her to count the various shapes.

Variations: Ask your child to write down how many snack mix pieces there are for each shape. Have her tell you which shape has the most, which has the fewest, and which, if any, have an equal number.

👁 Visual learners will enjoy visual comparison of shapes, so extend the activity to see if she can visually predict which shape has the most. Ask your child to predict which pile of sorted snack mix has the most of its shape and then ask her to count the shapes and keep a score sheet by making a tally mark on paper for each piece. Have her count the tally marks, write the number, and compare the number with what your child predicted.

 Kinesthetic learners can line up the shapes in rows and count them.

👂 Auditory learners can describe the shapes and count them out loud.

Mastery occurs when: your child can divide the snack mix according to shape.

You may want to help your child a little more if: she is having trouble sorting the shapes. Try using a smaller amount of snack mix in the activity. Once your child has sorted this amount, pour another small amount of mix onto the plate for her to sort. Continue until the cup of snack mix has been completely sorted.

5 | Identifying Shapes

Prepare a graph by folding the construction paper into fourths lengthwise. Label each of the four sections of the page with a different shape—square, triangle, rectangle, and circle.

Learning happens when: your child makes a graph of the different shapes he finds in old magazines. Ask your child to look through old magazines and cut out items that are similar to the shapes on the graph. Then ask him to glue the items down in the appropriate section of the graph.

Variations: Ask your child to count the shapes, write the numeral, and compare the results using "more than," "fewer than," or "equal to."

- 👁 Have your visual learner compare and contrast the various shapes as he describes them.
- 🖐 Kinesthetic learners should look through their toys for shapes and identify triangles, squares, rectangles, and circles.
- 👂 Ask your auditory learner which magazine he found each shape in and have him count the number of each shape out loud.

Mastery occurs when: your child can find shapes in the pictures of a magazine and can glue the shapes in the appropriate section of the graph.

You may want to help your child a little more if: he is having trouble finding the shapes. This task may overwhelm your child. If so, break it down into manageable parts. Ask him to find and cut out only circles. Once your child has found several circles, ask him to glue them on the graph. Continue searching for the shapes while focusing on one shape at a time.

TIME: 20 minutes

MATERIALS
- old magazines
- scissors
- glue
- construction paper
- marker

6 | Size Order

TIME: 20–30 minutes

MATERIALS
- 12 paper plates
- 4 different colors of markers

Divide the paper plates into four groups of three plates each. Using one group of plates and one marker, label the three plates with the following titles: Small, Medium, and Large. Take another group of three plates, and use a different colored marker to label them Big, Bigger, and Biggest. Use a third color of marker to label the next set of plates Small, Smaller, and Smallest. Finally, label the last set of plates Long, Longer, and Longest with the last marker.

Learning happens when: your child hunts for items around the house and puts them in order by size or length. Lay one set of plates out on the table. Ask your child to search for three items of different sizes. Put the small item on the Small plate, the medium item on the Medium plate, and the large item on the Large plate. Do the same thing for the other groups of plates.

Variations: Ask your child to glue pictures cut out from old magazines on the appropriate plates.

- Visual learners may prefer using the magazines in the variation to complete this activity.
- Kinesthetic learners can represent graduated size through movement. Ask your child to take a small step, then a medium step, then a large step, and so forth.
- Ask your auditory learner to talk about the items she finds and the reasons for their placement on the three plates.

Mastery occurs when: your child can order items according to size.

You may want to help your child a little more if: she is having trouble finding items to place on the plates. In this case, pick the items yourself and ask your child to put them on the appropriate plate.

7 What Time Is It?

Create a clock face on one of the paper plates by writing the numbers around the edge of the plate. Cut two arrows out of the second paper plate, making one of the arrows longer than the other. The arrows will be the hands of the clock. Color the arrows black. Use a hole punch or carefully poke a hole in the center of the clock and at the nonpointed ends of the hands. Poke the brad through the hands and then through the center of the clock. Turn the clock over and flatten the arms of the brad. Prepare the index cards by writing one hour on each of the cards (12:00, 1:00, 2:00, and so on).

Learning happens when: your child shows a given time on the clock. Review with your child how to show the time on the hour, reinforcing that the longer hand points to the twelve and the shorter hand to the hour. Shuffle the index cards and place them facedown on the table. Ask your child to draw a card and use the clock to show the time that is written on the card. If your child is correct, he scores a point. If he is incorrect, show him the correct time. Continue until all the cards have been played.

Variations: Try this activity in reverse. Lay the index cards faceup so that all the cards are visible. Make the clock show one of the times from the cards and ask your child to pull the card that shows the time on the clock. Continue until all the cards have been picked.

- 👁 Visual learners can practice writing down the time that the clock shows.

- ✋ Kinesthetic learners can use their arms to show the position that the clock hands should be in.

TIME: 15 minutes

MATERIALS
- 2 paper plates
- black marker
- brad (brass-colored paper fastener)
- 12 index cards
- scissors
- hole punch

 Your auditory learner can read the time aloud as he looks at the clock and the card.

Mastery occurs when: your child can create any time to the hour.

You may want to help your child a little more if: he is having difficulty creating a given time on the clock. Demonstrate to your child how to show the time. Give your child the opportunity to practice without the index cards by calling out a time and asking him to show it on the clock. Once your child can comfortably do that, introduce the index cards.

8 Coin Race

TIME: 15 minutes

MATERIALS
- small paper plate
- marker
- paper clip
- sharpened pencil
- several pennies, nickels, dimes, and quarters
- large sheet of construction paper

Prepare the spinner by drawing a vertical and a horizontal line through the center of the plate, dividing the paper plate into fourths. Each section of the plate will represent a coin. Draw a circle in the center of each section of the plate and write the first letter of the name of the coin in the circle (P = penny, N = nickel, D = dime, and Q = quarter). Prepare the graph by dividing the construction paper into fourths lengthwise. Label each section of the graph with the coin designations used on the plate.

Learning happens when: your child plays a spinner game and creates a graph of coins. Be sure to review with your child which coins match which letter on the spinner. You may want to talk about how a penny starts with the p sound, so the circle with a P stands for a penny. Continue the discussion with the other coins. Once your child understands, ask her to spin the spinner. The spinner works by spinning the paper clip around the tip of the pencil. To do this, place the paper plate down on a hard, flat surface. Next, place the paper clip on the spinner, making sure the center of the spinner is visible through one end of the paper clip.

Hold the point of the pencil on the center of the spinner and inside one end of the paper clip. The pencil should be perpendicular to the spinner, and the pencil should be holding the paper clip on the spinner. As you hold the pencil, ask your child to spin the paper clip. She may need to practice, but should be able to make the paper clip spin several times around the spinner. Once the paper clip has stopped spinning, ask your child to look at the section in which the paper clip is resting. She will then pick the correct coin that was spun and will place it in the appropriate section of the graph. Do this several more times. Once you and your child have spun ten to fifteen times, ask her to count how many coins are in each section of the graph.

Variations: Once your child has counted the number of coins in each section, help her count how much money is in each section. This may be tough for your child, but by doing it with her, you are modeling how to count money.

- 👁 Visual learners can use colors when making the graph for the activity, using red for dimes, blue for pennies, and so on.
- ✋ Your kinesthetic learner can see how the coins look when she stacks similar coins and can compare stacks by placing them side by side.
- 👂 Auditory learners can clap once for each coin in each group. Your child will hear which row contains the most coins.

Mastery occurs when: your child can identify the different coins and put similar coins together on a graph.

You may want to help your child a little more if: she is having trouble knowing which coin is showing on the spinner. Tell your child the name of the coin. See if your child can find the coin you have specified. If your child is having trouble recognizing the different coins, practice with two types of coins. Start with pennies and nickels. Those are usually the first two coins studied in school. Flip a coin. If it is heads, your child is to pick a penny out of the coin collection. If it is tails, ask your child to pick a nickel out of the coins. Continue playing until your child can successfully distinguish pennies and nickels. Then introduce the dime. Once your child can distinguish pennies, nickels, and dimes, introduce the quarter.

9 | I Like Your Suit

TIME: 15 minutes

MATERIALS
- four paper plates
- marker

On the first paper plate, draw a heart; on the second, draw a diamond; on the third, draw a spade; and on the fourth, draw a club. Shuffle the cards.

Learning happens when: your child divides a deck of cards into suits. Ask your child to put all the heart cards on the plate with a heart, the club cards on the plate with a club, and so on.

Variations: For the more competitive child, introduce a stopwatch. Tell your child you will be timing to see how fast he can complete the task. Say, "On your mark, get set, go!" Alternately, competitive children may enjoy racing with you or a sibling.

- 👁 This activity is great for visual learners. They will probably find this task easier than the other types of learners do.

- ✋ Kinesthetic learners like the physical aspect of working with the cards and should practice shuffling the cards by stacking and restacking them several times.

- 👂 Encourage your auditory learner to say "heart," "club," "spade," or "diamond" as he places the card in the proper pile.

Mastery occurs when: your child can successfully divide a deck of cards into suits.

You may want to help your child a little more if: he is having trouble categorizing the cards. Ask your child to first put all the red cards in one pile and all the black cards in a second pile. Then lay out the heart and diamond plates and ask your child to divide the red cards according to suit. Do the same thing for the black cards and the club and spade plates. Once your child can work with two categories, try completing this task with all four plates and all the cards mixed together.

Environmental Learning

You will have many opportunities to reinforce math skills on a daily basis. As you are driving around town you can have your child identify numbers on signs. Count with your child in a rhythmical beat. When your child wants to buy something, tell her how much it is, give her a dollar, and ask if that's enough money to buy it. Make the most out of every opportunity, and your child will be learning without even realizing it.

End of Kindergarten Math Checklist

Students who are working at the standard level at the end of kindergarten:

____   Understand that numbers are symbols that tell you how many

____   Know about time and can tell time to the nearest hour

____   Recite numbers one through twenty corresponding to flash cards

____   Combine and separate sets using objects

____   Classify and sort sets

____   Solve addition facts through 10

____   Compare more, less, and same

____   Recognize half of a whole object

Kindergarten Science

8

Although it may be difficult to imagine kindergartners in lab coats performing experiments, science is an important part of the kindergarten curriculum.

Kindergarten science can be divided into two broad categories: science processes and science concepts. Science processes include these activities:

- Investigating and experimenting with objects to discover information

- Observing, describing, sorting, and classifying objects according to what they have in common

Beginning of Kindergarten Science Checklist

Students who are working at the standard level at the beginning of kindergarten:

___ Ask questions about how things work

___ Notice there are changes in the weather

___ Can identify some things that are the same and some things that are different in some objects

___ Can identify some things found in nature

___ Knows the concept of living and nonliving things

- Communicating questions, making predictions, and making observations orally, and/or in drawings

Science concepts your kindergartner will study are in the areas of physical, life, and earth and space sciences.

Physical science concepts include these activities:

- Describing and sorting objects using the five senses

- Comparing the properties of objects, such as objects that float versus objects that sink

- Studying how objects move—slide, turn, twirl, or roll

Life science concepts include these activities:

- Examining whether something is a living or nonliving thing
- Learning about the needs that plants and animals have in order to grow and observing the changes they go through
- Describing how animals move

Earth and space science concepts include these activities:

- Learning about the properties of common earth materials, such as soil, water, and rocks
- Observing and describing the daily weather and the four seasons
- Describing ways to conserve natural resources

In the kindergarten classroom, science is often integrated with other subjects through themes. For example, in the fall your child may be studying a unit about pumpkins. The teacher might read books about pumpkins for the language arts component of the curriculum. In the area of math, your child may measure a pumpkin's circumference using a roll of adding machine tape and cutting the strip so that it fits around the pumpkin. In science, your child may plant pumpkin seeds to study how plants grow. Even though kindergarten teachers integrate science with other subjects, there are still specified science processes and concepts that are being taught.

Science Processes

Every grade level has similar science processes that continue to build on each other through the grade levels. Your child has probably already been exploring science processes as a preschooler. Was "Why?" your child's most frequent response as a three- and four-year-old? As exhausting as an endless string of questions can be, your child was actually developing a skill that will be required in science: the ability to ask questions and to wonder about things. Your child's kindergarten teacher will be channeling that wonder and those questions into a useful skill set through science activities.

Many kindergarten science activities are designed to engage your child's communication skills, channeling the questioning that comes naturally to children toward questioning that is designed to engage learning. Your child will be taught to make observations and predictions and then to decide, through further observation, if predictions are right.

The two big processes in kindergarten science are classification and simple experiments. Although your child has experience with classifying, the process will be more intentional and refined. Your child may be given a group of items and asked to classify them in some way, or he or she may be asked to look at pictures of certain items and tell what they have in common. Many kindergartners find it easier to classify a hodgepodge collection of items into categories that make sense than to look at a grouping of items and tell what they have in common. Finding commonality among objects is a skill that does not come easily for some children. These children will need many opportunities to practice this skill set.

Your child will also be performing simple experiments. Many of these experiments may be performed in a center. The experiment may be testing objects to see if they float or if they sink or to see if they are magnetic. Because science in the kindergarten classroom is really an extension of children's experimentation with the world around them, these experiments will help your child make sense of the world and prepare him or her to explore more sophisticated concepts in the later grades.

Science Processes Skills	Having Problems?	Quick Tips
Observes, sorts, and classifies objects according to their common properties	Has trouble finding commonalities among objects	Give your child every opportunity to sort items around the house. For example, when putting away the clean dishes, ask your child to put the flatware away. You probably have one of those flatware organizers, where the dinner fork has a slot, the knife has a slot, the salad fork has a slot, etc. Putting away the flatware will require that your child sort the pieces by common properties. Alternatively, the laundry provides a golden opportunity for sorting and classifying. When faced with a pile of clean laundry, ask your child to make a pile of towels and a pile of sheets or a pile of shirts and pile of pants. This task can be adapted to any load of laundry. Your child may need guidance and help at first, but he should be sorting and classifying like a pro in no time.
Participates in simple experiments to discover information	Does not discover information from simple experiments	Your child is experimenting constantly. The trick is to learn from the experimentation. If your child is having problems learning from her experiments, you may need to provide a little guidance. This may entail stating the obvious connection you see between what your child is doing and what the results are. For example, if your child is playing with her cars in the kitchen, you may say, "Wow, when you push that car across the kitchen floor, it goes really far. Why doesn't it go as far in the den?" We hope your child will make the connection that the flooring material affects how the car moves. Once you help guide your child to make those discoveries with you, she will eventually be able to make those discoveries on her own.
Asks questions and predicts the answer	Asks questions but wants you to tell him the answer	Instead of answering all your child's questions, return some questions with a question in return. Ask your child such questions as "I'm not sure. What do you think?" Draw the prediction out of your child and then help him verify whether the prediction is right or wrong.
Makes observations about objects she sees	Has a hard time describing things she sees	Try playing the observation game I Spy with your child. Use lots of adjectives that include color, size, and texture.

Science Processes Activities

1 Button Sort

Learning happens when: your child sorts the buttons into groups. Give your child the buttons and explain to him that some of them go together and some do not. Ask him to find the buttons that have something in common and put them on a paper plate. Your child will probably sort by color first. Have him explain to you how he determined which buttons went together. Your child may have difficulty explaining his thoughts to you, but communicating them is an invaluable skill. After your child has sorted the buttons one way, ask him to sort them in a different way. Some kindergartners may be able to do this; others may have difficulty. Don't worry if your child has trouble with this activity. Sorting is a skill that is developed through practice.

Variations: If your child can do the activity easily, you may want to group them yourself and ask your child to explain how they are sorted. Do this a few times with the buttons sorted in different ways. The skills required to determine how objects are sorted are a little more advanced than the skills required to group common items.

👁 Visual learners will examine the buttons very closely and notice details that escape others. Ask your child to describe the details to you.

✋ Kinesthetic learners will enjoy the physical aspect of sorting the buttons. Ask your child to stack the buttons, arrange them according to shapes, and place them side by side when sorting.

TIME: 10–15 minutes

MATERIALS
▪ collection of 15–20 mismatched buttons
▪ paper plates

🙉 Auditory learners will benefit from a discussion of how they choose their sorting method. Ask your child lots of questions about sorting while he is completing the activity.

Mastery occurs when: your child can sort the buttons in two different ways.

You may want to help your child a little more if: he is having trouble knowing where to start. Suggest a way to sort the buttons. There are many ways the buttons can be sorted, such as by color, by size, by the number of holes in them, or by the material of which they are made.

2 Leaf Collecting

TIME: 30–45 minutes

MATERIALS
▪ leaves
▪ construction paper (one sheet for each group of leaves)
▪ glue
▪ marker

Learning happens when: your child collects leaves and then analyzes and sorts the collection. Go on a nature hunt with your child, collecting ten to fifteen different types of leaves. After the leaves have been collected, ask your child to divide the leaves into groups according to things they have in common. After the leaves are divided, ask your child to explain why she grouped the leaves in this manner. Decide on titles for each group of leaves ("Big Leaves," "Sharp Leaves," "Round Leaves," and so on). Write the title at the top of a sheet of construction paper. Ask your child to glue the leaves that fit in that category. Do this for each group of leaves.

Variations: Make a book of leaves. Have your child author the book by dictating the words that you'll write on the page.

👁 Visual learners will most enjoy the second half of this activity. Extend this portion of the activity by providing your child with crayons, markers, or glitter so that she can decorate the leaf posters. Find a place to display her handiwork.

✋ Kinesthetic learners will enjoy being outdoors collecting and sorting the leaves, so extend the activity by collecting nuts, twigs, and other things from outside.

👂 Auditory learners will benefit from a discussion of how the leaves were sorted. Ask her to tell you more details about the leaves and why she placed them in her groups. You can expect to hear more from an auditory learner than from other learners.

Mastery occurs when: your child can classify the leaves in a way that makes sense.

You may want to help your child a little more if: she is having trouble classifying the leaves. You may want to guide your child by stating an observation about a leaf. For example, "This leaf is made of a bunch of little leaves. Are there other leaves like this one?" Once you and your child have found the ones that are similar, make another statement about a different type of leaf. Continue with the rest of the collection.

3 | Toy Sort

Learning happens when: your child works with you to organize his toys. This is an especially good activity if your child's toys are disorganized or thrown together in a heap. Decide how you want the toys organized (cars in one container, dress-up clothes in another container, coloring books in a third, and so on). Label each container and have your child go through his toys and put the appropriate toy in the appropriate container. Once your child's toys are organized, help him maintain the system by putting things away in their appropriate containers each evening.

TIME: 30 minutes

MATERIALS
- your child's toys
- various containers
- marker

Variations: Toys can be sorted by use or frequency of use. For example, one container can be for things your child plays with daily and another for things your child plays with less frequently.

👁 Visual learners will be pleased with the organization element to this activity. Try using colored containers or labels when sorting the toys.

✋ A kinesthetic learner will remember how to keep his room organized better if you let him put the containers of toys in the place where they go.

👂 Your auditory learner will respond to talking about why he wants to put certain toys in certain spots. Ask him lots of questions about his choices, such as "Why are you storing your games there?"

Mastery occurs when: your child can successfully sort the toys by some attribute.

You may want to help your child a little more if: he is having trouble sorting. Guide your child by asking questions. For example, "What do you have in your hand? Which tub do you think it needs to be put into?"

4 Bouncy Egg

TIME: 10 minutes

MATERIALS
- large jar
- egg
- vinegar

Learning happens when: your child changes the properties of an eggshell by soaking it in vinegar. Gently place the egg in the jar. Pour vinegar into the jar until the egg is completely covered. Ask your child to observe what is happening. (She should notice the bubbles coming off the egg.) Leave the egg in vinegar for one day. The next day, take the egg out of the vinegar. Ask your child to touch the egg and describe how it has changed. She should notice that the eggshell is now soft. This happens because of a chemical reaction that occurs when the eggshell comes in contact with the vinegar.

Variations: Use a hard-boiled egg for this experiment. Once the shell has softened in the vinegar, leave the egg out in the air for a day. What happens now? The egg should get very hard. Alternatively, if you used a raw egg for this experiment, place the softened egg into water and watch as the water is absorbed into the egg until it breaks open.

- 👁 Visual learners will notice the bubbles coming off the egg and other small changes other learners may not notice. Ask your child to record the changes by drawing pictures of the egg before, during, and after soaking.

- ✋ Kinesthetic learners will enjoy feeling the results of this experiment. Ask your child to think of at least one other thing that feels the same way.

- 👂 Auditory learners may want to discuss their findings with you. Ask your child to describe the experiment to you a day or two after you complete it.

Mastery occurs when: your child understands that things can change. Your child may not understand why or how the vinegar changed the egg, but she should understand that the vinegar caused the change in the egg.

You may want to help your child a little more if: she does not see the difference in the egg. Pull out a regular egg. Ask your child to feel both the egg soaked in vinegar and a regular egg. Ask her to describe how they are different. Follow up by asking your child what was done to the vinegar egg that was not done to the other egg. This should help your child better understand the changes that occurred.

Physical Science

Description will be a big focus when learning about physical science. Your kindergartner will be using the five senses—sight, sound, taste, smell, and touch—to describe and sort objects. Sight will probably be used more than any of the other senses, but your child will need to be able to describe things by attributes other than how they look. For example, your child may be asked to describe how something smells, or he or she may listen to sounds and be asked whether the sounds are loud or soft. To reinforce this skill, ask your child to describe things to you in daily life. If your child is tasting a new food, ask him or her to tell you what it tastes like. By asking your child to describe something, you are reinforcing skills that extend beyond the science classroom. Description requires a depth of thinking that will help your child in language arts and math as well as science.

In addition to describing and sorting using the five senses, your child will be asked to compare the properties of objects. For example, he or she may be asked to compare objects to see which are magnetic and which are not. A simple way to reinforce and extend this set of skills is to highlight key properties in one object and ask your child to think of other objects that have the same properties. For example, you might say, "This hose is long and flexible. Can you think of something else that is like this hose?"

Finally, your child will be exploring how objects move. Objects move in different ways. Some objects roll, like balls and wheels. Other objects, such as the hands on a clock, move by turning. A carousel moves by twirling, and pulling a hose causes it to move by sliding. You can help your child understand this concept by commenting on how things are moving. Over time, your child will notice and comment independently on the movement of objects.

Physical Science Skills	Having Problems?	Quick Tips
Observes, describes, sorts, and classifies objects by their sensory attributes, such as how they sound, how they feel, or how they look	Has trouble describing objects using the five senses	Constantly ask your child to describe things in your environment. This can be as simple as asking what a candle smells like (like a strawberry or a flower), asking what a food item tastes like (sweet, chocolaty), asking how a sweater feels (soft, itchy), etc. Describing is a learned skill that requires practice. You can also show your child how to perform this skill by describing things you see, feel, smell, etc. Remember that your child is always watching and learning from you.
Compares and describes the properties of objects	Has trouble comparing objects	Ask your child to compare objects around the house. Start by comparing only two objects. For example, you may ask your child which grocery bag is heavier, which jacket is warmer, etc. After your child can easily compare two objects, ask her to compare more than two objects.
Observes and describes how objects move	Has trouble remembering the different types of movement	It can be very confusing trying to remember the difference between a slide, twirl, turn, and roll. Start with one movement. Ask your child to think of things that move in that way, or go on a hunt around the house for things that move in a particular way. Once your child is comfortable with one movement, talk about a different one. Continue in the same way until your child understands the four basic movements.

Physical Science Activities

1 Finding Objects

TIME: 15–20 minutes

MATERIALS
- sheet of construction paper
- old magazines
- scissors
- glue
- marker

Learning happens when: your child uses the sense of sight to locate pictures that meet a certain criteria. Write the title "Round Things" at the top of the sheet of construction paper. Ask your child to look through magazines to find pictures of things that are round. Once your child finds a picture of something that is round, ask him to cut out the picture and glue it to the mini-poster. This activity will require that your child use his sense of sight to categorize objects.

Variations: This activity can be used for any visual clue. For example, you may want to have your child cut out pictures of blue things or things that are triangular.

👁 Visual learners will probably be very good at using visual clues to categorize, so try adding another requirement; for example, ask him to find round things that are blue.

✋ The kinesthetic learner will enjoy the cutting and gluing aspect of this activity, and you can add to it by asking your child to collect some things from around the house that meet the criteria but won't be glued onto the poster. Stack some of the things around the poster and leave it for a few days.

👂 Auditory learners may need to think out loud, so you should ask your child about what he is looking for. Demonstrate thinking out loud by saying things under your breath, such as "Something round, mmmm . . . something round; well, that is round, I like that, cutting out something round . . ."

Mastery occurs when: your child can use visual clues to locate things that fit in a category.

You may want to help your child a little more if: he is having trouble finding items. Practice a few with your child. If your child wants you to verify if a picture fits, ask your child what he thinks. Guide him without doing the activity for him. Once your child is able to find a few on his own, he should be able to work more independently.

2 Hear the Music, Feel the Music

Learning happens when: your child uses the sense of hearing to categorize songs as fast or slow. Grab a few of your favorite CDs and your child. Play a song for her and ask her whether it is a fast or a slow song. It is up to you whether or not to listen to the whole song. Try this activity with a few more songs. After a while, your child will be able to quickly categorize the song as fast or slow.

TIME: 15–20 minutes

MATERIALS
- collection of various types of music

Variations: If your child loves to dance, have her dance with quick steps to fast songs and move slowly to slow songs. Alternately, you can use other categories, such as happy songs and sad songs or loud songs and soft songs.

- 👁 A visual learner will benefit from turning your radio controls so that she can see the LCD panel moving to the beat of the music. This can almost always be seen from the bass or treble settings on your radio.

- ✋ Kinesthetic learners will enjoy doing the dance variation to this activity.

This activity is perfect for an auditory learner because it taps into her strength, but you can reinforce it by asking your child to clap to the beat of each song to see if she hears more or less clapping to fast or slow songs.

Mastery occurs when: your child can use hearing to categorize music as fast or slow.

You may want to help your child a little more if: she is having trouble telling the difference between songs. Try the dance variation. Your child may find it easier to move with the music rather than just to listen to the music.

3 Blind Taste Test

TIME: 15–20 minutes

MATERIALS
- several bite-size pieces of food
- blindfold

Learning happens when: your child identifies food using the sense of taste. Have several bite-size pieces of food available, but out of your child's sight. For example, you could have a small marshmallow, a piece of banana, a spoonful of peanut butter, a piece of celery, and a bite of hard-boiled egg. Blindfold your child. Put one of the pieces of food into your child's mouth. You should feed your child, so that he does not use clues from touching the food to tell what it is. Ask your child to identify the food. Continue until all the pieces have been used. Be sure to use food with which your child has experience.

Variations: Ask your child to plug his nose as you feed the bites. This will make it more difficult, as he is not relying on clues from his sense of smell.

Your visual learner can describe what the food looks like after he describes how it tastes. If he doesn't know what the food is, lift the blindfold to show him what it looks like. Visual learners may also like to describe what something tastes like by using a "color": hot is red, grape is purple, and so on.

✋ After your kinesthetic learner identifies the food, ask him to tell you how the food feels on his hands and in his mouth.

👂 Auditory learners should describe the taste well and how they feel about the taste.

Mastery occurs when: your child can use taste clues to identify foods.

You may want to help your child a little more if: he is having trouble identifying a food. Ask questions about the food to help your child narrow down the list of potential candidates. For example, if your child is having trouble identifying celery, ask him if the food is sweet or not sweet. Then ask your child what are some things it could be. Continue narrowing it down. Do not worry if he cannot identify each food. The point of this activity is to use a sense (taste) that your child usually does not use to identify items.

4 | Touch and Guess

Learning happens when: your child uses the sense of touch to identify items in a bag. Put the items into the bag. Ask your child to close her eyes, reach into the bag, and feel around until she finds an object. See if your child can identify the object, which might be a spoon, an unsharpened pencil, a ball, a small cup, a small toy, or the like. See how many items your child can identify. For those that your child cannot identify, provide a clue.

Variations: Ask your child to close her eyes and find a particular item among the objects in the bag. For example, ask your child to find the pencil.

TIME: 10–15 minutes

MATERIALS
▪ collection of various items that have different textures
▪ large, opaque bag

👁 Visual learners may be tempted to peek, but no peeking! You can let your child see the object after she guesses what it is or has described the way it felt and tried to guess what it is. If your child failed to accurately identify the object, then it is especially important to show her what it is.

✋ Kinesthetic learners will probably find this activity fairly easy because it plays to their strengths. Make the activity harder by trying to use objects that are similar in feel with only slight distinctions, such as an unsharpened pencil and a straw.

👂 Auditory learners should describe what they are feeling while they are feeling it. Ask your child to tell you about every detail of the object.

Mastery occurs when: your child can rely on the sense of touch to identify objects.

You may want to help your child a little more if: she is having trouble identifying objects. Try the variation. See if your child can find a particular object first. Then put the same objects back into the bag and ask your child to feel and identify each object, with no clues from you.

5 | Floaters or Sinkers?

TIME: 15–20 minutes

MATERIALS
- collection of several items, some that float and some that do not
- large bowl or bucket of water
- 2 paper plates
- paper towels
- marker

Learning happens when: your child tests items to see if they float or sink. Draw a simple picture of a boat on one plate. Explain to your child that a boat floats, so any item that floats will go on that plate. Draw a picture of an anchor on the other paper plate. Explain to your child that an anchor sinks, so any item that sinks will go on that plate. Gather several items. Examples of some items around the house that float include a cork, a marshmallow, and any item made of Styrofoam. Examples of some household items that sink include a penny, a spoon, and a pencil. Ask your child to predict which items will float and which will sink. Then ask him to test whether or not he is right by gently placing each item in the water. After testing each item, dry it with a paper towel and place it on the correct plate. When finished, ask your child if he was surprised by any of the floaters or sinkers.

Variations: Some items can float if they are put on the water very carefully, but will sink if they are put into the water a different way. For example, a paper clip may float if gently placed on the water so that it is in a flat position. If it is turned vertically, however, it will sink. Experiment with items to see if any of them can be both floaters and sinkers.

👁 Your visual learner will enjoy categorizing the items, so it would be good to have him make a simple chart by placing an S(inker) and F(loater) at the top and a line down the middle. Your child should make a mark for each item that floats or sinks using a different color for each item.

 The kinesthetic learner should help you collect a few small things to test. Ask your child to help you set up for the experiment and to help you put things away when you are finished. This demonstrates the entirety of the activity and gives your child an opportunity to think about what he wants to learn and then about what he has learned in the setup and clean-up process.

👂 Auditory learners may benefit from thinking aloud. Ask your child to count as things sink to "time" how long it takes them. Let him lightly touch the things that are floating to see them bounce back up. Talk about why some things float and some don't.

Mastery occurs when: your child can test an item and tell whether it floats or sinks.

You may want to help your child a little more if: he is having trouble completing the activity. Test a few items with your child. Talk about what you are doing and think out loud as you determine whether an item floats or sinks. As your child sees you do it, he will want to do it himself.

6 Movements

TIME: Two 20-minute sessions

MATERIALS
■ 8 index cards
■ marker
■ fairly large open area

On each index card, write one of the following eight objects: mop, zipper, hands of a clock, doorknob, spinning top, merry-go-round, ball, and tire. Shuffle the index cards and put them aside.

Learning happens when: your child determines how an object moves, and then performs a motion that represents that movement. Teach your child the movements: sliding, turning, twirling, and rolling. To show a slide, take a sideways step and slide one leg across the floor until it is next to the other leg. To show a turn, ask your child to do a cartwheel. If your child cannot do a cartwheel, ask her to draw a large circle in the air with her index finger. To show a twirl, ask your child to put her arms out and turn one complete circle. Finally, to show a roll, ask your child to do a somersault. If your child cannot do a somersault, ask her to lie on the floor and roll around one time, from tummy to back to tummy again. Once your child has learned the movements, call out the name of a movement to test your child. Do this a few times to make sure she can perform the specified movements on command. Once your child has mastered the movements, explain to her that objects each have their own movement. Read an index card to your child and explain to her that you want her to think of how the object moves and to perform the movement that goes with the object. The zipper and mop slide. The doorknob and the hands of a clock turn. The spinning top and merry-go-round twirl. The ball and tire roll. Draw a card and read the object. Ask your child to slide, turn, twirl, or roll to show how the object moves. This activity may be best performed in two separate sessions. Teach your child the movements during the first session and introduce the index cards at the second session.

Variations: You can extend this activity by asking your child to find other things in the house that move. Ask your child to describe or perform the movement.

👁 Visual learners may need to see how the object moves before being able to perform the movement. Start the activity with movements for objects whose movement you can show to your child (clock hands, bouncing ball, zipper, and so on).

✋ Kinesthetic learners will enjoy the active nature of this activity and will excel because it taps into their natural abilities. Try combining one movement with another by drawing two cards at one time.

👂 Auditory learners may need to describe the movement either before she does the activity or while she is doing it.

Mastery occurs when: your child understands that objects move in different ways, and can describe or show how the object moves.

You may want to help your child a little more if: she is having trouble determining the movement. This activity will probably be difficult for many children. You may need to use the actual objects to demonstrate how they move before your child does the activity. Alternately, you may want to perform this activity once with your child and then ask your child to perform the movements independently. Do not worry too much if your child has difficulty with this activity. The main idea is that objects move in different ways.

Life Science

Your child will be exploring plants and animals in life science. The first concept that kindergartners will learn is that some things are living and some are nonliving. Most kindergartners already understand this intuitively because of their experiences as preschoolers; the learning will be a little more formal in this grade level. Kindergartners will look at what plants and animals need to stay alive, how animals move, and the stages of life that plants and animals go through.

To help your child learn about the needs of living things, ask him or her to help you take care of any pets or plants you may have. Discuss

Life Science Skills	Having Problems?	Quick Tips
Distinguishes between living and nonliving things	Has trouble telling the difference between living and nonliving things	Start by helping your child understand that plants, animals, and people are living things. Ask him to list as many plants, animals, and people as possible. Once he understands this, add insects to the list of living things. Most children intuitively understand the difference between living and nonliving. If your child does not understand the difference, start small and build from there.
Understands the needs of living things	Does not understand that there are certain needs all living things have in order to survive	Relate the needs of other living things to the needs of your child. She will probably recognize that she needs food and water to survive. Explain that other living things need food and water as well. Asking your child to help take care of plants and pets will reinforce the idea that living things have needs.
Understands that living things go through stages	Does not understand the different stages in the lives of living things	Talk with your child about the changes he has gone through. Pull out the baby pictures. Talk about how your child has grown. Relate this to you. Pull out your baby and childhood pictures. Talk about how all people go through stages. Once your child understands the stages people go through, extend the idea to plants and animals. Books are a great resource, with wonderful pictures that show the stages of life.

the need for water as you give water to a pet or as you water a plant. Talk about how animals and plants need food just as people do. Taking care of other living things is an excellent opportunity to reinforce an understanding of the needs that living things have.

To help your child understand the different stages of life, check out some animal books from the library. Your child will love looking at the photographs and can learn a lot just by looking at them. If possible, you may want to consider a trip to your local zoo, aquarium, or farm. This is a great opportunity for your child to see animals that he or she isn't able to see in daily life.

Life Science Activities

1 Living or Nonliving?

Learning happens when: your child makes mini-posters that show the difference between living and nonliving things. At the top of one of the sheets of construction paper, write the title "Living." At the top of the other piece of paper, write "Nonliving." Ask your child to go through the magazines. Have him cut out pictures of living things and place them on the Living poster and cut out pictures of nonliving things and place them on the Nonliving poster. After your child has several pictures on each poster, discuss his choices. Ask him how he decided where to place the pictures. Be sure to talk about any pictures that he placed on the wrong poster. Ask your child leading questions that will help him correctly categorize the picture. After the discussion, ask your child to glue the pictures on the posters.

Variations: Use twenty index cards. Ask your child to cut out ten pictures of living things and ten pictures of nonliving things.

TIME: 20–30 minutes

MATERIALS
- two sheets of construction paper
- old magazines
- scissors
- glue
- marker

Make sure each picture will fit on an index card. Glue each picture to a card. After the cards are dry, shuffle them and place them facedown. Ask your child to turn them over and make a pile of living things and a pile of nonliving things. For a more competitive child, you can time him with a stopwatch.

- A visual learner could add more decoration to his poster—for example, by including additional pictures of living and non-living things. The point is to ask this learner to demonstrate more visually—whether by adding more items or more details to the poster.

- The kinesthetic learner will enjoy cutting the pictures and gluing them to the mini-poster. Ask your child to tell you how the things on the poster move. Does a rock move? Does a car move? How does a tree move? Living and nonliving things move. Talk about how this happens and ask your child to demonstrate.

- Your auditory learner should tell you how he is making the decision to categorize something as living or nonliving.

Mastery occurs when: your child understands the difference between living and nonliving things.

You may want to help your child a little more if: he is having trouble telling the difference between living and nonliving things. Discuss what he should look for when finding pictures of living and nonliving things. You may want to review the differences between them. Seeing how you do it and hearing you think aloud will help your child understand the thought process behind successfully completing this project.

2 | Germination Bags

Learning happens when: your child watches a seed germinate. Get a couple of large seeds, such as dried beans or pumpkin seeds. If you are using dried beans, soak them in water overnight to encourage germination. Ask your child to moisten a paper towel. It needs to be very moist, but not sopping wet. Fold the paper towel into fourths and put it into the plastic bag. Lay two or three seeds in the bag on top of the paper towel. Seal the bag. Place the bag in a safe place where it will receive some light. Ask your child to observe the seeds daily for a couple of weeks. The seeds should germinate fairly quickly. Discuss the changes your child sees each day. At the end of the experiment, you and your child can plant the seed in a container or outside.

Variations: Give your child a small notebook. Ask her to draw what the seed looks like each day. Some kindergartners will do very well with drawing what they see, whereas others may struggle with this task.

- 👁 Visual learners will benefit most by trying the variation to this activity.

- ✋ The kinesthetic learner will enjoy creating the germination bag and should definitely plant the seed after it germinates.

- 👂 Auditory learners will benefit from discussing the changes they see. Ask your child to dictate a description of the changes to you each day. Write your child's description down and ask your child to draw a picture to go with it.

Mastery occurs when: your child understands that a seed grows into a plant.

TIME: 10 minutes for prep

MATERIALS
- 2 or 3 large seeds
- zipper-style plastic sandwich bag
- moistened paper towel

You may want to help your child a little more if: she is having trouble understanding the point of this activity. Discuss with your child how the seed will grow into a plant. Make sure that your child talks to you about the changes she sees. Discussing the germination of the seed will help your child understand what she is witnessing.

3 Animal Movements

TIME: 20–30 minutes

MATERIALS
- 12 index cards
- marker

Write the following animals on individual cards: dog, cat, turtle, snake, worm, snail, frog, rabbit, grasshopper, bird, butterfly, and bat.

Learning happens when: your child mimics the movements of an animal to show whether that animal crawls, walks, hops, or flies. Before introducing the index cards, teach your child the movements. To represent walking, your child will walk. To represent crawling, he will get down on his hands and knees and walk on all fours. To represent hopping, your child will squat and leap like a frog. To represent flying, he will flap his arms. Have your child practice the movements by showing them to you.

After your child has demonstrated that he can perform the movements, shuffle the index cards and place them facedown. Draw a card and read it out loud. Ask your child to think about how the animal moves and then mimic the movement by using one of the motions he practiced. The dog, turtle, and cat are walkers. The snail, worm, and snake are crawlers. The frog, rabbit, and grasshopper are hoppers. The bird, butterfly, and bat are fliers. Continue until all the cards have been used.

Variations: Ask your child to think about other animals that can be added to the cards. Make index cards for those animals. Play the game again, using the new cards as well as the old ones.

👁 Ask your visual learner to imagine the animal's movements before mimicking them.

✋ This activity caters to the strengths of kinesthetic learners; you can increase the difficulty of the activity by asking your child to demonstrate more than one movement at a time.

👂 Auditory learners can make the sound that the animal makes while doing the movement.

Mastery occurs when: your child can show you the different ways in which animals move.

You may want to help your child a little more if: he is having trouble determining how an animal moves. Ask your child to move like the animal. Is that movement closer to a walk, crawl, hop, or fly? Talk with your child about how various animals move from place to place.

4 | Stages of Life

If you like to draw and can render clear pictures for your child, you can draw these stages. If not, you can easily use pictures you find at www.knowledgeessentials.com. On three of the cards, draw a picture of each of the following: seed, sapling, and tree. On another three index cards, draw a picture of each of the following: seed, small plant, and plant with flowers. On another three index cards, draw each of the following: egg, baby bird, and adult bird. On the last three index cards, draw each of the following: baby, child, and adult.

TIME: 15–20 minutes

MATERIALS
- 12 index cards
- markers

Learning happens when: your child organizes cards that show the stages of life for four different organisms. Shuffle the index cards and place them facedown. Ask your child to turn over the cards and match them into four groups of three. Once your child has divided them into groups of three, ask her to arrange each of the groups in order from youngest to oldest. This may be a fairly challenging activity for your child, so be sure to ask her leading questions that will help her match the cards and arrange them.

Variations: You can play a variation of Concentration with the cards. Remove the seed card, egg card, and baby card. Put the other cards facedown in a grid arrangement. Take turns turning over two cards at a time. If the stage shown on the cards matches the organism, that player takes the cards and goes again. If the cards do not match, the cards are turned back over, and play goes to the other player. The person who makes the most matches wins.

- 👁 Visual learners will benefit from seeing the cards in order. Ask your child to draw the stages of life for something else, such as a puppy and a dog. Don't worry if there are only two stages.
- ✋ The kinesthetic learner will enjoy working with the cards, but you can also ask her to act out the stages after the cards are put in order.
- 👂 Auditory learners may need to discuss their choices and think out loud. Ask your child many questions about the cards to help her think through the activity.

Mastery occurs when: your child understands that living things change as they grow, and can put the cards in proper order.

You may want to help your child a little more if: she is having trouble matching groups that go together. Arrange the cards into groups for your child and then ask her to put the cards in order from youngest to oldest. Do this several times, until your child is able to group the cards and put each group in order.

Earth and Space Science

Much of your kindergartner's time in earth and space science will be spent exploring the weather. In fact, many kindergarten classrooms will have some sort of daily activity regarding weather. Your child will be keeping track of what the weather is like each day—cloudy, rainy, sunny, and so on. He or she will also be exploring the four seasons, particularly the different weather patterns that occur during each season.

Earth and Space Science Skills	Having Problems?	Quick Tips
Understands the properties of common earth materials	Cannot describe common earth materials	Ask your child to help with the gardening, so that she can get her hands in the dirt. Working with the soil will help your child understand its properties. Look for pretty rocks with your child and start a collection with her. Alternately, some science stores will have beautiful rocks and minerals for sale. You may want to visit one and allow your child to buy one or two. Talk with her about where water is found on the earth. Take a trip to a nearby lake, river, or ocean. Do some water activities with your child. Firsthand experiences with these earth materials will help your child understand their properties.
Describes the daily weather	Cannot describe the daily weather	Have a quick daily discussion with your child about the weather. Go outside with him to observe the weather. Discuss whether the sky is cloudless, partly cloudy, or filled with clouds. Talk about the temperature, whether it is hot, warm, or cold. By having these discussions, you are showing your child how to describe the weather. Before long, he will be giving you the scoop on the weather.
Observes and describes the characteristics of the four seasons	Does not recognize the characteristics of the various seasons	Discuss the four seasons with your child. Describe the characteristics of each one. For example, you may comment on the pretty fall leaves or how the summertime is so much fun because it is warm enough to swim. Use the season words when talking about the changes you see.

Your child will also be studying the properties of common earth materials. Kindergartners will be looking at things found in nature, such as water, soil, and rocks. Your child will be examining the different earth materials and describing their properties.

Finally, your child will begin studying how to conserve natural resources. Kindergartners will study how items can be recycled or reused in other ways. You can easily reinforce these concepts at home with simple "activities," such as saving water by taking showers instead of baths or not running the water while brushing your teeth. Your child will learn about saving electricity by turning off the lights in rooms that are not being used.

Earth and Space Science Activities

1 Leaf Rubbings

TIME: 15–20 minutes

MATERIALS
- collection of several types of leaves
- paper
- crayons

Learning happens when: your child makes rubbings of the different types of leaves, discovering the shape and texture of these materials. Gather five or six leaves of different shapes. Place a leaf on the table and place a piece of paper on top of the leaf. Peel the paper off the crayon. Hold the crayon horizontally and firmly rub the crayon back and forth across the paper over the leaf. The texture of the leaf should show through. Make sure the crayon stays horizontal. Continue with the other leaves, using different colored crayons, if desired.

Variations: You can make rubbings of many different textures, such as the trunk of a tree or the surface of a large, flat rock.

👁 Visual learners will learn by noticing the details in the finished product. Ask your child to describe the details of the rubbings, including the similarities and differences among them.

👋 The kinesthetic learner will learn through the process of creating the rubbings. Ask your child to lightly rub his fingers over the sheet while it is still on top of the leaf. Can he feel the similarities and differences when using the crayon versus feeling the lumps with his hand?

👂 Auditory learners should notice the way it sounds to make a rubbing and how the object underneath the paper changes the way it sounds. Try asking your child to make rubbings of very different things and then to describe their sound and how they look.

Mastery occurs when: your child understands that there are many different types of leaves that have different shapes and different textures.

You may want to help your child a little more if: he is having trouble making the rubbings. Make sure your child is holding the crayon horizontally when making the rubbing. It will not work if the crayon is held the conventional way.

2 Rock Collection

Learning happens when: your child looks for different types of rocks. Take a nature walk with your child in a local park or in the neighborhood. Ask your child to look for interesting rocks. If there is a river nearby, there may be some good finds along the bank. Make sure it is safe to walk near or along the bank, and watch your child at all times. When you and your child have collected a few interesting rocks, discuss your finds. Ask your child to

TIME: 20–30 minutes

MATERIALS
▪ place to display the rocks

describe what the rocks look like. Which rocks look similar, and which look totally different? What color(s) does your child see? Display some of your child's favorite rocks.

Variations: Arts and crafts stores have rock polishing machines for sale that are designed for the amateur rock collector. If your child really enjoys collecting rocks, you may want to consider one of these machines for a birthday gift.

- 👁 Visual learners will notice more visual details about the rocks, so you should ask her to categorize them based on their visual characteristics.

- ✋ The kinesthetic learner should describe how the rocks feel. Ask her to categorize the rocks based on how they feel.

- 👂 Auditory learners will want to talk about their finds, so ask your child to tell you about the details of the rocks, particularly the similarities and differences.

Mastery occurs when: your child understands that there are different types of rocks and can describe their properties.

You may want to help your child a little more if: she is having trouble describing the rocks. Ask your child to describe the rock by color first. Some rocks have flecks of different colors. Does your child notice any color variations? Ask her whether the rock is rough or smooth. What about the shape? By guiding a discussion with leading questions, you are showing your child the different characteristics of rocks and how to describe them.

3 | Earth Materials Match-Up

Prepare the index cards before beginning. On one index card, write "Water" and draw a picture of water. On the second index card, write "Soil" and draw a picture of a flower growing in the soil. On the last index card, write "Rock" and draw a picture of rocks.

TIME: 15–20 minutes

MATERIALS
- 3 index cards
- colored markers or crayons

Learning happens when: your child plays a game that matches an earth material with clues about that material. Spread the three index cards out on a table. In random order, read the clues listed here. Ask your child to hold up the card that fits the clue. Make sure to mix the clues up. Continue until you have read all the clues.

Water clues: (1) Fish swim in me. (2) People and animals drink me. (3) I sometimes fall from the sky.

Soil clues: (1) Plants grow in me. (2) Earthworms live in me. (3) Add water to me, and I become mud.

Rock clues: (1) Mountains are made of me. (2) People sometimes skip me across a lake. (3) Some buildings are made of me.

Variations: For competitive children, assign points. Give your child one point for each correct answer. See how many points your child can accumulate. For children who really understand this concept, ask them to make up their own clues to test you.

👁 Visual learners may want to help you create the cards. Write the word on each index card and ask your child to draw the corresponding picture below it.

👋 The kinesthetic learner can benefit from helping you collect physical examples of the earth materials. Fill plastic containers with rocks, soil, and water and then let your child place the index card by the container that holds the earth materials you describe.

👂 Auditory learners will benefit from adding more spoken clues about the earth materials. You can even try making the clues harder.

Mastery occurs when: your child can match the clues to the earth material.

You may want to help your child a little more if: he is having trouble matching the clues. Guide your child through the first round. Ask leading questions that will help him reason through the clues. After helping your child for a round, do another round to see if your child can independently match the clues to the correct earth material.

4 Weather Swat

TIME: 15–20 minutes

MATERIALS
- 3 paper plates
- colored markers
- clean flyswatter

Prepare the paper plate before starting. On the first paper plate, write "Hot and Sunny" and draw a picture of the sun. On the second plate, write "Rainy" and draw a picture of raindrops falling from a cloud. On the last plate, write "Snow" and draw a picture of a snowflake.

Learning happens when: your child matches special clothes and equipment to the appropriate weather. Call out a piece of clothing or equipment and ask your child to use the flyswatter to swat the plate that describes the weather best suited for that piece of clothing or equipment. For example, if you call out "umbrella," your child should swat the Rainy plate. The clothing and equipment are as follows:

Hot and sunny: sunglasses, bathing suit, shorts

Rainy: umbrella, raincoat, rubber boots

Snow: coat, gloves, scarf

Be sure to mix up the words you call out. Call out one word at a time and have your child swat the appropriate plate. Continue until all the items have been used.

Variations: Competitive children may want to get a point for each correct answer. Your child may be able to think of other items; you can be the swatter as your child calls out items. If you have two or more children, they might want to play together to see who can swat the plates first. Make an additional set of plates for each child.

- 👁 Visual learners should help you draw the pictures on the plates and can add pictures of the clothing items to the plates at the end of the game.

- ✋ For your kinesthetic learner, you can hold up a plate and ask her to put on the clothes that she would wear in that kind of weather.

- 👂 Auditory learners can tell you about a time when they wore each clothing item and what the weather was like that day.

Mastery occurs when: your child is able to match items to the correct weather plates.

You may want to help your child a little more if: she is having trouble matching the clothing and equipment to the weather. Talk it through with your child. Do a few together until she gets the hang of it.

5 | Four Seasons Concentration

TIME: 15–20 minutes

MATERIALS
- 8 index cards
- 4 paper plates
- colored markers

Label each of the paper plates with the name of a different season. On the eight index cards, draw or glue a picture of the following things: a snowflake, snowman, swimming pool, bathing suit, rosebud, rose, pumpkin, and jack-o'-lantern.

Learning happens when: your child plays Concentration and matches the pairs to the appropriate season. Mix the index cards and place them facedown in a grid pattern. Your child will turn two cards over. If they are a match, he will then put the pair on the appropriate season plate. The pairs and seasons are as follows: winter—snowflake and snowman; summer—swimming pool and bathing suit; spring—rosebud and rose; fall—pumpkin and jack-o'-lantern. If the player makes a match and places the pair on the appropriate plate, that player takes another turn. If the player makes a match but places the pair on the wrong plate, then the index cards are turned over and placed back on the grid, and play goes to the next player. If there is no match, then the next player takes a turn. Continue until all the matches have been made and placed on the appropriate plates.

Variations: Play a game of Concentration that matches the season to an object. Prepare an index card for each season and omit the plates. For example, the eight cards would be summer and bathing suit, fall and pumpkin, winter and snowflake, and spring and rose. Simply play Concentration with these eight cards instead.

👁 Visual learners should help decorate the plates and the cards. Ask your child to decide what some of the pictures should look like.

✋ After your kinesthetic learner makes the matches, ask him to place the cards in a pattern, such as summer-fall-winter-spring or winter-spring-summer-fall.

👂 Auditory learners should tell you about something he did in each season.

Mastery occurs when: your child can match the cards to the appropriate season.

You may want to help your child a little more if: he is having trouble matching and then categorizing according to season. Complete the Concentration portion of the game. In other words, only make the matches. Then, once the matches have been made, discuss with your child where each card should go. Your child will learn more about the seasons through this type of discussion.

Environmental Learning

Your child's natural curiosity is the kernel needed for a good science investigation. The world is full of things to observe, describe, identify, and wonder about. When you're out grocery shopping, observe your shopping cart. How does it move when it's inside the store? Does it move differently when you're in the parking lot? Observing and talking about these concepts while your child can see them in action is the most effective way to help him or her fully understand them.

Discuss the weather and the seasons with your child. Comment on the changes you see as the weather or the seasons change. Ask your child what changes he or she notices.

Ask your child to help recycle in your house. If you are not currently recycling, start with aluminum cans. Get a separate trash bin only for cans. Ask your child to take on the responsibility of rinsing and putting the cans into the recycling bin. When it is full, take the cans to the nearest recycling center. By participating in the effort, your child will learn more about recycling than by just talking about it.

End of Kindergarten Science Checklist

Students who are working at the standard level at the end of kindergarten:

____ Investigate and experiment with objects

____ Observe, describe, sort, and classify objects

____ Participate in simple experiments to discover information

____ Communicate questions, make predictions, and make observations orally and/or in drawings

____ Describe and sort objects using the five senses

____ Compare the properties of objects, such as objects that float versus objects that sink

____ Identify how objects and animals move—slide, turn, twirl, or roll

____ Identify whether something is living or nonliving

____ Understand needs that plants and animals have in order to grow and the changes these organisms experience

____ Understand the properties of common earth materials, such as soil, water, and rocks

____ Observe and describe the daily weather and the four seasons

____ Understand and describe ways to conserve natural resources

Kindergarten Social Studies

Guess what? You're a social studies teacher, and you might not have even known it! You've been your child's primary teacher up to this point, teaching your child to share, take turns, and follow family rules. If you celebrate any holidays, you've been teaching social studies and culture. These traditions become a part of your child's cultural heritage.

Kindergarten social studies teaches children about the world they live in and their place in it. Kindergartners will focus on the self, home, family, and classroom. Personal connections make social studies more meaningful to your child. For this reason, many kindergarten classes begin their social studies learning with a unit on "Me." A "Me" unit stresses the unique individual and commonalities among people in general.

In addition to learning about themselves, children will be learning about civics, history, and geography. These may sound like advanced topics for your little kindergartner, but don't let the technical names put you off—it's really all about the people, places, things, and events your child comes across every day.

Anything that happened in the past is history! Your child will be learning a broad basic history through the stories of historical events, important Americans, and people and events honored by holidays. Learning about history helps your child understand how this country evolved and appreciate the people and events that helped in its creation.

Holidays

What with the celebrations, the decorations, and the family traditions, holidays are always a great time for children. Holidays are more than just fun, however; they're also part of your child's social studies curriculum.

Holiday celebrations are as unique as the people and culture that celebrate them. People in England celebrate Christmas differently from

Holiday Skills	Having Problems?	Quick Tips
Knows there are different ways to celebrate holidays	Thinks that if someone is celebrating a holiday differently, it must be a different holiday	Relate the cultural differences in holiday celebrations to something your child can understand. Sporting events are a good example. Each team has different colors, a different mascot, a different cheer, etc. That doesn't change the game they are playing, just as celebrating a holiday differently doesn't change the holiday.
Names some of your family's holiday traditions	Doesn't identify any particular way your family celebrates any holiday	Talk to your child about what holidays you celebrate. Do you take a vacation every Christmas? Do you go to a picnic every Independence Day? Do you make valentines on Valentine's Day? Remind your child of this and explain what a tradition is. You can have old and new traditions, so don't limit yourself in this discussion!
Knows reasons why we celebrate some holidays	Doesn't connect historical events or traditions with holiday celebrations	Check out library books that tell about the history of different holidays. Examples can be found at www.knowledgeessentials.com. Talk about the background of the holidays as they occur.

people in the United States. It may not occur to your child that many holidays are celebrated differently in other parts of the world, because your child's learning up until this point has been very close to home.

Holidays are a great topic because they open up your child's eyes to a multitude of cultures and countries around the world. Discussing new places, religions, and people helps your child understand that not everyone and everything is the same and that that's a good thing. Diversity is the spice of life!

Holiday Activities

1 | My Very Own Calendar

This activity is a good one to start on the first day of the month. You may want to do this activity every month with your child.

Using the pencil and ruler, create seven columns and five rows on the large sheet of paper, leaving room at the top for the month. Ask your child to help you label each column with the days of the week—not to write them. Say to your child, "What is the first day of the week? Sunday, yes, that's right. What day comes after Sunday?" It is important to talk about what you are writing when you write it because that reinforces your child's efforts to read and write. Take a look at the printed calendar and fill in the numbers for each of the days. Put the month at the top of the calendar. Use the opportunity to reinforce science skills by talking about what kind of weather happens during that month.

Learning happens when: you and your child talk about the holidays your family celebrates throughout the year. Make sure you include national holidays. Because some of these fall on different dates each year, you may want to look at a calendar that lists them

TIME: 15–20 minutes

MATERIALS
- large sheet of paper
- pencil
- ruler
- markers and crayons
- calendar

for that year. Ask your child to think of holidays that are in that month. Talk with your child about each one and then help him draw and label it on the calendar you've made. You can definitely add important family events, such as birthdays, but make sure to stress that there's a difference between holidays and other celebrations or events.

When the calendar is filled in, hang it up in your child's room. It's a great way to reinforce the month, day, date, and any important holidays or family events. And it's something you can do every month!

Variations: If a month is too much planning to do all at once, use a weekly calendar.

- 👁 Creating the calendar is perfect for a visual learner. Being able to look at the calendar every day is a great visual tool that helps your child work not only on social studies skills but also on math and language arts. If your child wants to make calendars for the entire year at once, go for it!

- ✋ For a kinesthetic learner, making a calendar might not be enough. You may want to get, or make, a supplemental calendar that requires changing daily, such as a block calendar that needs to have the date changed or a daily calendar that needs to have a page removed.

- 👂 This is a great activity for auditory learners. Discussing the holidays and family events that occur in each month helps your child identify important days. Creating the calendar for your child to look at only helps reinforce that.

Mastery occurs when: your child can identify holidays by memory or by using the calendar.

You may want to help your child a little more if: he cannot identify any holidays. Start off with the big commercial holidays. It's hard to miss the patriotic red, white, and blue theme that's everywhere for the Fourth of July. Or start out with the holidays that are in your child's birthday month, as he is more apt to know about the holidays in the month he was born.

2 Independence Day and the American Flag

Learning happens when: you look at and discuss the importance and symbolism of the American flag with your child. Explain what the parts of the American flag symbolize—the stars are for each of the fifty states, the stripes for each of the thirteen original colonies.

TIME: 30 minutes

MATERIALS
- *F Is for Flag,* by Wendy Cheyette Lewison
- crayons
- paper
- American flag

Read *F Is for Flag,* by Wendy Cheyette Lewison. Talk with your child about the story and about what the flag represents to many Americans. Connect the flag to Independence Day by talking about why we celebrate this holiday.

Ask your child to draw the American flag on a sheet of paper. While she is drawing, ask questions about what you've been talking about, such as what the parts of the flag symbolize, to check for understanding.

Variations: This activity can be used for any holiday by changing the book and the holiday symbol.

👁 Visual learners will especially benefit from the book used in this activity and from looking at a real flag. While you're out and about with your child, ask her to point out examples of the flag. See if you can find an older flag with fewer stars, and ask your child why it's different.

✋ A kinesthetic learner would love to touch a flag! If you don't already have one, get one and let your child help you put it out in the morning and take it down in the evening.

👂 For auditory learners, the book in this activity is a perfect way to teach your child about the American flag and its importance.

Mastery occurs when: your child can identify the American flag and knows basic facts about it.

You may want to help your child a little more if: she is having difficulty picking out the flag. You may want to show your child the flags of some other countries to show how each flag is unique. The American flag is the only one with fifty stars and thirteen stripes. Be sure to point out the flag when you're out—there's bound to be one at every municipal building and school in your town.

3 | President's Day

Time: 45 minutes

Materials
- *Abe Lincoln: The Boy Who Loved Books,* by Kay Winters
- *If You Grew Up with George Washington,* by Ruth Belov Gross
- paper
- crayons
- pennies, nickels, dimes, and quarters

Learning happens when: you talk with your child about President's Day and its significance. What does a president do? Who is the current president? Who was the first president?

Show your child the coins. Discuss who is on each coin, focusing primarily on George Washington on the quarter and Abraham Lincoln on the penny. Read the two books with your child and then talk about them. What were some important facts about George Washington's life? What about Abraham Lincoln's? Ask your child why he thinks people consider them good presidents. Give your child the crayons and paper and help him illustrate something about one of the two presidents that he heard in the book.

It is important to start introducing American history in little pieces, so don't think that this introduction to Washington and Lincoln is the moment to tell your child all about the Revolutionary and Civil Wars. The point that you are trying to make at this age is that there are people who have done things in history that affect the way we live today.

Variations: If this seems to be too much information in one sitting, try this activity for just one president at a time.

- For visual learners, find photos and other visuals about the presidents to supplement the books. The book *Don't Know Much About the Presidents,* by Kenneth C. Davis, has a *great* wealth of information that can grow with your child as he becomes a reader.

- Give your kinesthetic learner the opportunity to explore by going to a history museum. If there isn't one nearby, check out your local library or schools around President's Day— they often have displays set up for children.

- To enhance this activity for your auditory learner, you may want to ask him to talk about what he found out about the presidents and why we celebrate President's Day.

Mastery occurs when: your child can identify George Washington and Abraham Lincoln as two presidents of the United States and talk about some of the things each is famous for.

You may want to help your child a little more if: he has a difficult time remembering who Washington and Lincoln are. Ah, money—it's one of the world's most frequently used bribes. Of course, in this case you can use it as more of a learning tool than a bribe. The next time your child asks for money for an item or for his allowance, try this: if the amount is under a dollar, ask your child for a fact about Abraham Lincoln and then give the amount in pennies; if it's over a dollar, ask for a fact about George Washington and then give the amount in quarters.

4 Thanksgiving

TIME: 30 minutes

MATERIALS

■ any book about the history of Thanksgiving, such as *The Night Before Thanksgiving,* by Natasha Wing, or *The Story of Thanksgiving,* by Nancy J. Skameas

■ large sheet of paper

■ crayons

Learning happens when: you and your child discuss the meaning of Thanksgiving. What does your family do for this holiday? Is it a big shindig with extended family and friends or a small family affair? Ask your child to share her favorite part of the holiday. Although most kids will say the food is their favorite part of the holiday, and it *is* a great part, it's important for your child to understand where Thanksgiving comes from.

Read the story about the history of Thanksgiving with your child. Discuss the pilgrims that came to America and the Native Americans who helped them find food in their new home and prepare their first feast. Talk about the foods that are commonly associated with the first feast. Ask your child what your family usually serves at Thanksgiving. What is your child's favorite dish?

After your child has chosen her favorite food, help her create her own picture recipe for it. Use the large piece of paper as a big index card. (Let's hope your child has chosen a food that isn't *too* involved or *too* simple.) Ask your child to draw pictures of ingredients she recognizes. Then use those drawings in the directions. On Thanksgiving, you can ask your child to help you create that part of the meal using the picture recipe!

Variations: Ask your child to try this activity, but make a dish that she thinks is a favorite of a family member.

👁 A visual learner will love creating the recipe for this activity. You can use the activity as it is, and if your child is feeling particularly artistic, feel free to ask her to illustrate either the first Thanksgiving as described in the book or some other part of the book that she may have found interesting.

Kinesthetic learners might like to take their new picture recipe for a trial run! It's never a bad idea to practice before the big holiday, so get your little cook into the kitchen and ask her to help use the recipe you both created. And while you're at it, review with your child what the holiday was like during the first feast.

Your auditory learner might prefer to dictate the recipe rather than draw it out on paper. While you're working, make sure to review what you've been learning about Thanksgiving.

Mastery occurs when: your child can identify some of the facts about Thanksgiving and the foods associated with the holiday.

You may want to help your child a little more if: she has trouble remembering facts about the history of Thanksgiving. Create a turkey body from brown construction paper and cut out a dozen feathers from different colors of paper. Every day before Thanksgiving, come up with a fact that you and your child can write on one of the feathers. Glue or tape the feather to the body. By the time Thanksgiving arrives, you'll have a turkey with beautiful and informative tail feathers!

Neighborhoods and Community Helpers

The large majority of kindergarten social studies revolves around things that are close to home—literally and figuratively. Kindergartners spend a lot of time learning about themselves and each other, what is in their neighborhood and community, and how everything relates to them. Geography is no exception, consisting of locating and describing familiar places and beginning to understand the concepts of city or town, state, and country.

Learning about community helpers, such as police officers, firefighters, doctors, and nurses, teaches kindergartners about responsibility and about how these individuals and others help people in their neighborhood.

Neighborhoods and Community Helpers	Having Problems?	Quick Tips
Understands that people live together in communities	Has trouble understanding the concept of a community	Talk about the parts of your community in your daily life. Point out ways that people in a community help each other. What are some of the things that people in a community share? What are some of the things they do together?
Identifies features in your neighborhood	Can't tell your neighborhood apart from any other	Take a walk around your neighborhood and talk about the places in it where people live and kids play. Are there places to shop in your neighborhood? Is there a school in your neighborhood? A park? Try "thinking aloud" by saying things like "There's the yellow house with the birdbath in the yard; we're almost home."
Identifies some of the people in the community who help others	Doesn't distinguish between people who are helpers in the community from all others in the community	Helpers can many times be identified by uniforms, so talk about what police and doctors wear to work. Another way to pick out community helpers is by where you find them. Doctors and nurses work at doctors' offices and at hospitals. Teachers work at schools. Police officers can be found at the police station and out and about in the community.

Neighborhoods and Community Helpers Activities

1 Home Collage

Learning happens when: you and your child talk about where you live. Are there lots of cars? Lots of buildings? Maybe there are lots of cows or sheep? Is there a police station nearby? A shopping center? Talk with your child about the different types of communities there are—towns, cities, and the country. What kind of community do you and your child live in?

Go through the magazines and newspapers with your child while she chooses images that relate to your community. Glue these to the construction paper to create a community collage. Review how the different people and objects shown in the collage relate to your community.

Variations: Make a collage of a different community, such as the one where your child's grandparents or other family members live.

TIME: 30 minutes

MATERIALS
- magazines and newspapers
- scissors
- glue
- construction paper

- If this activity doesn't seem to be enough for your visual learner, go out into your community and find the things that make it a town, a city, or the country.

- Your kinesthetic learner might benefit from a walk around the community as well. Take your child to the local market, walk through a park, check out some of the tall buildings downtown, or find a farm with a petting zoo.

- For your auditory learner, be sure to discuss each type of community in depth. While out and about, ask your child to tell you what he sees in the neighborhood and to identify the type of community you're driving through.

Mastery occurs when: your child can tell you what type of community he lives in and how he knows that.

You may want to help your child a little more if: he has difficulty identifying the community he lives in. You may want to start by pointing out different things that are unique about the community you live in. Then discuss how these different aspects of your community make it one of three special kinds of communities. Start off by just discussing *your* community. Then, as your child gets more comfortable with this first type of community, introduce one of the other two types and continue until your child can identify each type of community and some of its characteristics.

2 | Transportation

TIME: 30–45 minutes

MATERIALS
▪ *Cars and Trucks and Things That Go,* by Richard Scarry
▪ construction paper
▪ crayons

Learning happens when: you talk to your child about transportation. Ask your child if she has heard the word before and what she thinks it might mean. Talk about how you get from place to place. Do you walk everywhere? How do you get to school every day? Don't forget to mention such modes of transportation as buses, taxis, planes, trains, and boats.

Read the story *Cars and Trucks and Things That Go,* by Richard Scarry. In addition to the great story and wonderful illustrations about transportation, your child gets the chance to search for Gold Bug on each and every page!

After reading and discussing the story with your child, ask her to draw a form of transportation she likes from the story.

Variations: Change the topic to forms of communication and talk about how people communicate with each other using telephones, e-mail, text messages, and letters. Look for relevant books at your library, such as *Clifford the Big Red Dog: The Big Red Dog Telephone Book*, by Brooke Hessel (Christopher Moroney, illustrator).

- 👁 If your child is a visual learner, the book will definitely help get the concept of transportation across, but you can also take a walk or a drive around town and get a firsthand look at different types of transportation in your community.

- ✋ If your child is a kinesthetic learner, it's time to take a trip! Take a walk, take a bus or a taxi, take a horseback ride or maybe a train ride. This is a great way to make her drawing come alive! Your child will enjoy seeing a mode of transportation she has never seen before, so be creative!

- 👂 Auditory learners will benefit from talking with you about transportation and listening to the story, so this activity is already geared for your child.

Mastery occurs when: your child can identify different types of transportation.

You may want to help your child a little more if: she cannot name different types of transportation. Don't get too broad too quickly. Start off close to home with things like walking, bicycling, and driving the car. Then start to add new forms of transportation one at a time. Or start with transportation on land, then move to sea and then air.

3 | My Address

TIME: 20 minutes

MATERIALS
- photograph of your home
- index card
- marker
- paper
- crayons

Learning happens when: you and your child take a look at the photo of your house or apartment to see if your child can see the address number. If it is visible, ask your child to tell you the numbers. If it isn't visible, write out the address number on an index card. How many numbers are in your address number? Ask your child if he also knows the name of the street you live on. Discuss with your child why homes have numbers and why it's important to know them.

Ask your child to draw a picture of his home. When your child is finished, help him write the house number and street address underneath it.

Review this activity with your child over the next few days by asking him to tell you his address.

Variations: Try a version of this activity with your phone number. Instead of a picture of the house, just draw a picture of a phone.

- 👁 Visual learners can do this activity just as it is! They will benefit from seeing the photograph of the house and drawing a picture of it with the address.

- ✋ If you have a kinesthetic learner, try making the house out of clay or wooden sticks—and don't forget to add the address number on it.

- 👂 An auditory learner will learn best by talking about his address, so reviewing it verbally every day will help your child remember it. When you are filling out paperwork, such as at a doctor's office or when applying for a store credit card, ask your child to help you by telling you the address.

Mastery occurs when: your child can tell you his address from memory.

You may want to help your child a little more if: he has trouble remembering his address. Try coming up with a short rhyme or song to help your child remember, or find ways to associate the numbers with other familiar things. For example, if your address is 14 Maple Street, you might say that another way to remember it is that your child's sister is fourteen and there's a maple tree outside the house. I know not everyone will have it that easy, but I'm sure you can come up with *something!*

4 Community Helpers

Learning happens when: you ask your child about the people in the community who are there to help others. Who helps at school? Who helps around the town? Who helps in an emergency?

Read the book to your child. Afterward, talk with her about some of the community helpers you might not have discussed before. Ask your child to draw a picture of one of the community helpers either from the book or in your own town.

Variations: Name a community helper for your child to draw and then ask your child to dictate a story about the helper for you to write down.

👁 Be sure to show your visual learner the pictures in the book as you're reading. To review, go back and point at the pictures to see if your child can identify who each helper is.

✋ Ask your kinesthetic learner to act out some of the activities that certain community helpers do. Make it into a game of

TIME: 40 minutes

MATERIALS
- *Community Helpers from A to Z,* by Bobbie Kalman
- blank sheets of paper for drawing
- writing paper
- crayons
- colored pencils
- pencils

charades and see if you can guess what profession your child is acting out.

🦻 Auditory learners will benefit from listening to the story and discussing community helpers with you. Don't forget to ask questions that your child will know the answers to—it makes her feel that she has a firm grasp of the topic and will encourage her to continue talking.

Mastery occurs when: your child can identify a variety of community helpers.

You may want to help your child a little more if: she has difficulty understanding what a community helper is and what that helper does. Try taking your child to meet a firefighter or a crossing guard and letting your child see what job each person does in the community.

5 | Dentists

TIME: 30 minutes

MATERIALS
■ pictures of dentists and dental tools (most pediatric dentists provide these)
■ *The Berenstain Bears Visit the Dentist,* by Stan and Jan Berenstain
■ paper
■ crayons

Learning happens when: you talk with your child about the dentist. Show your child the pictures you have of dentists and the tools they use. Ask your child what he thinks a dentist does and what he or she uses the tools for. Your child will probably know what the toothbrush and toothpaste are for, but you'll have to explain the picks and mirrors and other tools.

Read the book with your child and then talk about what the dentist's job was in the story. How can you make sure your teeth are healthy? Discuss with your child the importance of good oral care: brushing twice a day, flossing, using mouthwash, and having regular visits to the dentist.

Brush and floss your teeth together.

Variations: Try this activity with other health topics, such as going to the doctor or eating healthy foods.

👁 Visual learners will get a lot out of looking at the illustrations in the book; you can also ask him to draw his own picture. Feel free to take your child on your next routine visit to the dentist so that he can see what goes on and how a dentist helps you take care of your teeth.

✋ The kinesthetic learner might like to pretend to be a dentist. Let your child examine your teeth, show you how to brush them correctly, and take good care of them.

👂 For your auditory learner, you may want to pair this activity with his routine visit to the dentist to find out what exactly dentists do with all those tools and how they help keep everyone's teeth healthy.

Mastery occurs when: your child can identify what dentists do, what tools they use, and how they can help keep people's teeth healthy in the community.

You may want to help your child a little more if: he cannot describe to you how dentists are important in the community. Talk with your child about how important it is to take care of your teeth. If you didn't have teeth, you couldn't chew your food! If people didn't have dentists to show them how to care for their teeth, people would lose their teeth and not be able to enjoy all the tasty foods there are to eat.

6 Police Officers

TIME: 20–30 minutes

MATERIALS

■ photo of a police officer

■ construction paper

■ markers

Before you start this activity, write the phrase "Police Officers Help the Community By . . ." on a few sheets of construction paper.

Learning happens when: you ask your child to look at the photo and tell you who that person is in the community. What does a police officer do to help people in the community? As your child verbally lists some police responsibilities, complete the sentence fragments on the sheets of construction paper. Once all the sheets have complete sentences, your child can illustrate them to create a short picture book of important things that police officers do in the community.

Variations: Try this activity with other helpers, such as teachers, doctors, or firefighters.

👁 The visual learner will benefit from illustrating the sentence pages you create together. Make as many as your child feels is necessary and then bind the pages to create a book your child can "read."

✋ A kinesthetic learner would do well to visit a police station and find out firsthand what a police officer can do. A lot of municipalities have programs to show kids what it's like to be a police officer, so check with your town hall.

👂 Auditory learners love to talk and listen, so browse your local library for books on police officers and the work that they do every day. Reading and discussing the books will help reinforce your child's learning.

Mastery occurs when: your child can identify a police officer and his or her roles in the community.

You may want to help your child a little more if: she is having difficulty thinking of things that police officers do in the community. You may want to go around your town and see if you can't find a police officer in action—helping out at a construction site, helping direct traffic, riding in the police car to help someone who may have had a car accident or is in another situation where he or she needs help. Obviously you don't want to interfere with any emergency work a police officer is involved in, but you might be able to chat with an officer on a break.

Rules and Safety

Civics may sound like a subject for high schoolers, but trust me, it's something that your child will be learning about *all* through school. Civics starts off in the home long before your child reaches kindergarten. I'm sure you've got house rules and consequences if they're broken. For kindergartners, civics is about understanding cooperative play and work, how to take individual responsibility for things, and learning about rules and procedures and why we need them to work and play safely.

Although it may not seem too much like social studies, learning the rules and procedures of the school day really *is* part of the subject. If you think about it on a larger, more national scale, this makes sense; learning the rules and regulations for school leads to learning the rules in society and breeds better citizens in the community.

All the rules and regulations in the school are made for safety. Following the rules generally leads to a safe environment, but sometimes accidents happen, and children, as well as adults, need to be aware of what to do. Fire drills, classroom safety, and basic first aid are also taught as part of your child's social studies curriculum in kindergarten.

Rules and Safety Skills	Having Problems?	Quick Tips
Follows the playground rules	Does not follow the rules on the playground	Read to your child the portion of the school handbook that pertains to school rules. Talk with him about the rules and the reasons for having them. Explain that it is important to follow the rules, and talk about the consequences of repeatedly breaking the rules.
Asks for help	Doesn't recognize the school helpers	Talk with your child about the way to ask a trusted adult for help. Role-play to practice the skill. Get a school annual and look through the pictures of the teachers and administrators with your child. Teach her the names of the teachers with whom she deals throughout the week.
Recognizes important environmental signs	Has problems finding his way around the school building	Point out important signs on the way to school with your child (Stop, Entrance, Exit, Restroom, Danger, etc.).

Rules and Safety Activities

1 Stop, Drop, and Roll!

TIME: 10 minutes

MATERIALS
- soft mat
- fire detector
- paper
- crayons

Learning happens when: you and your child talk about fire safety. What are some things that your child can tell you about fire? How would your child know if there was a fire in the house? What should he do if there is a fire? If your child doesn't already know about the fire alarm, show it to him. Explain what it's for and turn on the alarm so that your child can hear what it sounds like.

Ask your child what he would do if his clothes caught fire. Explain that it's a scary situation but that as long as he keeps calm and thinks about things, he can take care of the fire quickly and safely with the Stop, Drop, and Roll plan.

Talk with your child about how he should stop where he is (running around can make the fire spread quicker), drop to the ground, and roll back and forth to put out the flame. Demonstrate it for your child on the mat and then ask him to do the same, saying each word for each part of the plan.

After you and your child have finished practicing, ask him to draw each step on the paper. Label it for your child and then hang it somewhere in the house where it can be seen frequently to remind everyone!

Variations: Do this same activity for other emergency situations. If you live in the Midwest, practice tornado safety; if you live in California, practice earthquake procedures, and so on.

- 👁 For your visual learner, you may want to get a video from your local library or Red Cross that your child can watch.

- 🖐 This is already a great activity for a kinesthetic learner!

- 👂 Talk with your auditory learner about fire prevention more than once or twice. Ask your child to tell you about the Stop, Drop, and Roll plan. The more you discuss it, the more it will stick in your child's mind.

Mastery occurs when: your child can perform the Stop, Drop, and Roll plan.

You may want to help your child a little more if: he has difficulty remembering the drill. Practice, practice, practice! Try incorporating this into your child's morning routine—after he gets out of bed, ask to see how to Stop, Drop, and Roll.

2 | School Rules

TIME: 15 minutes

MATERIALS

- board game your child doesn't know the rules to
- paper
- pencil
- list of the rules in your child's school classroom

Learning happens when: you ask your child to explain to you what rules are. Discuss some of the rules that your child has to follow at home. Ask your child why she thinks your family has rules at home. (Answers will include "to keep us safe," "to keep things in order," "to make things a little easier.") What might happen if there were no rules? What happens when you break a rule at home?

Bring out the board game and ask your child to play it with you, but don't tell her the rules to the game. How difficult is it to play? Read the rules to the game with your child and then play a real game. Did the rules of the game make it easier?

After talking with your child about the rules at home, explain that there are rules to follow at school as well. Show your child the list of rules from her classroom. Read through them and talk about each one. Don't forget to mention the consequences if the classroom rules are broken.

Variations: Keep a chart to track how many days or times your child follows the rules.

- 👁 A visual learner might like to rewrite or even illustrate the classroom rules in a way that's more understandable to her. Help your child write them, making sure to keep the same focus in the rules.

- ✍ Kinesthetic learners can try acting out the rules in a Good Idea, Bad Idea skit. Choose a rule and perform a skit that demonstrates the incorrect way to act. Ask your child to perform a skit that demonstrates the correct way to follow the rules.

Your auditory learner will be hearing the classroom rules quite frequently during the first few weeks of school, so make sure you ask her to share them with you every so often when you're at home to see if she is remembering them.

Mastery occurs when: your child can identify classroom rules and their importance.

You may want to help your child a little more if: she has a hard time remembering the rules. Sometimes children are just forgetful, and the consequence for breaking rules doesn't always instill the correct behavior. You may want to review the rules on the way to school each morning or focus on one at a time, starting with whichever one your child may be having the most difficulty with.

3 The Signs of Safety

Before starting this activity, create a few pages of signs by drawing an outline of each sign on a sheet of paper and coloring it the appropriate color. Be sure you leave out the words or pictures in each sign, because your child will complete this in the activity. Some good ones to use are the Stop sign, the School sign, and the Exit sign. Use ones that would be found in your neighborhood and your town.

TIME: 15 minutes

MATERIALS
- *I Read Signs,* by Tana Hoban
- paper
- markers

Learning happens when: you read *I Read Signs* with your child and discuss with your child the signs he knows. Where can signs be found? Why are signs important? What do signs tell people?

Bring out the pages you have already made and let your child take a look at them. What is different about these signs as compared to the signs from the book? Using the book as a reference, ask your child to help you fill in each sign.

Variations: Incorporate other signals, such as traffic lights, crosswalk lights, sirens, and others.

- 👁 The visual learner will enjoy pointing out signs everywhere, so don't leap out of your seat when your child yells "STOP!" from the backseat when he sees a Stop sign.

- ✋ The kinesthetic learner would love to take a walk with you around the neighborhood to show you all the signs he can find. Go ahead and hunt for signs in the neighborhood, but remind your child that there are more signs indoors as well!

- 👂 An auditory learner will need to talk about the types of signs you see, so when you're out, ask your child to point out different types of signs. If he knows what the signs mean, ask him to tell you. If he doesn't, explain them to him.

Mastery occurs when: your child can identify different types of signs.

You may want to help your child a little more if: he has trouble remembering what the signs mean. Ask your child to use the sheets he has made as a reference. Play matching games. When your child finds a sign that he can't remember, look through the sheets to find it. If it's there, you can remind him what it means. If you haven't made it yet, go ahead and create another one with your child and discuss what it means.

Environmental Learning

It's nice knowing that you can teach your child all sorts of things that will be important in his or her social studies education. Social studies is a subject that is always relevant to where you are and what you're doing.

There are lots of chances in your day-to-day life to bring up social studies! Ask your child to show you around her school. Get directions from your child on the best way to get back home from school. Have your child point out some important community helpers on your way through town and, while you're at it, ask her to tell you where things are around the neighborhood.

Holidays are a great time to talk about family and friends and the special events they celebrate. Calendars are not only a great way to keep track of your child's busy schedule but also great tools for teaching your child about holidays, important events, and time management.

There are many ways to add social studies into your child's everyday learning, so go ahead and be a social studies teacher!

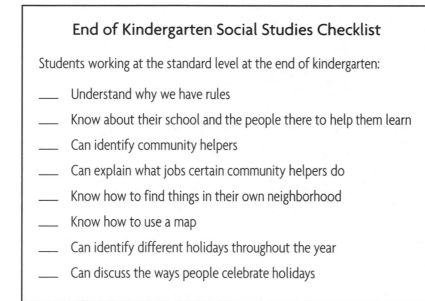

End of Kindergarten Social Studies Checklist

Students working at the standard level at the end of kindergarten:

___ Understand why we have rules

___ Know about their school and the people there to help them learn

___ Can identify community helpers

___ Can explain what jobs certain community helpers do

___ Know how to find things in their own neighborhood

___ Know how to use a map

___ Can identify different holidays throughout the year

___ Can discuss the ways people celebrate holidays

Teaching Your Kindergartner Thinking Skills

10

Teaching your kindergartner to think sounds like a lofty goal, doesn't it? You can help foster a thinking mind in your child by treating him or her as an active participant in a home where you explore "why" and "how" questions. The more opportunities your child has to explore ideas and be heard at home, the more likely he or she is to be an active thinker both in and out of school.

Teaching children to use reason and to think logically improves their impulsive behavior and social adjustment. Children taught this way are less likely to develop behavioral difficulties than are well-adjusted children who do not learn these skills. Of course, the way you respond to your child and act in front of her has the most significant impact on how she learns to think and communicate.

In a study of children from kindergarten through fourth grade (Shure, 1993) that was the culmination of twenty years of research to test ideas about thinking skills, parent modeling, and behavior, M. B. Shure delineated four levels of communication that we use all the time.

> ## Beginning of Kindergarten Thinking Skills Checklist
>
> Students who are working at the standard level at the beginning of kindergarten:
>
> ____ Communicate needs, wants, and thoughts verbally
>
> ____ Use complete sentences to recount an event
>
> ____ Ask questions
>
> ____ Follow two-step directions

LEVEL 1: POWER ASSERTION (DEMANDS, BELITTLES, PUNISHES)

- Do it because I say so!
- Do you want a time-out?
- How many times have I told you . . . !
- If you can't share the truck, I'll take it away so that neither of you will have it.

LEVEL 2: POSITIVE ALTERNATIVE (NO EXPLANATION)

- I'm on the phone now. Go watch TV.
- Ask him for the truck.
- You should share your toys.

LEVEL 3: INDUCTION (EXPLANATIONS AND REASONS)

- I feel angry when you interrupt me.
- If you hit, you'll lose a friend (hurt him).
- You'll make him angry if you hit him (grab toys).
- You shouldn't hit (grab). It's not nice.

LEVEL 4: PROBLEM-SOLVING PROCESS (TEACHING THINKING)

- What's the problem? What's the matter?
- How do you think I (she/he) feel(s) when you hit (grab)?
- What happened (might happen) when you did (do) that?
- Can you think of a different way to solve this problem (tell him/her/me how you feel)?
- Do you think that is or is not a good idea? Why (why not)?

The parents who communicated as often as possible on level 4 in Shure's study had children who were the least impulsive, were the least withdrawn, and showed the fewest behavior problems as observed by independent raters.

We all know that there are times when communicating on level 1 is the only way to go, so don't beat yourself up. You can't reason a child out of the street when a car is coming. Awareness of the communication levels enables you to implement the highest level as much of the time as possible, which in turn fosters a thinking child.

Teaching and modeling thinking encourages children to ask questions about information and ideas. It helps your child learn how to identify unstated assumptions, form and defend opinions, and see relationships between events and ideas. That you are even reading this book assures you are a thinking person, so you are on the right track.

Don't expect your child's kindergarten teacher to stand up in front of the class and say, "Okay, it's time to learn to think." Instead, he or she will incorporate activities and language that foster the development and refinement of thinking skills, such as problem solving, concentration, and reasoning, throughout your child's daily activities. In the same way, you will foster thinking skills if you do many of the activities in this book with your child.

There are many approaches to teaching thinking. You can teach your child to use a set of identifiable skills, such as deciding between relevant and irrelevant information and generating questions from written material. This is particularly useful for auditory and visual learners. Your kinesthetic child learns to think more actively by participating in sports, hands-on projects, and similar activities.

Problem Solving

Problem solving is a hallmark of mathematical activity and a major means of developing mathematical knowledge. It is finding a way to reach a goal that is not immediately attainable. Problem solving is natural to young children because the world is new to them, and they exhibit curiosity, intelligence, and flexibility as they face new situations. The challenge at this level is to build on children's innate problem-solving inclinations and to preserve and encourage a disposition that values problem solving. Try the math activities about patterns and the science activities about earth materials in this book as challenging opportunities for your child.

Concentration

Thinking skills begin with the ability to maintain a focus on one thing long enough to think it through. Thinking something through means understanding the information (in whatever form—for example, visual, print, or oral), questioning the information, and thinking about the alternatives before making a decision.

Concentration skills are a big part of learning to read. Your child's teacher will be working hard with him or her on concentration skills, and you can help reinforce these skills by trying the activities in the reading comprehension section of chapter 5.

Comprehension

This is a hard one. To think about something in a reasonable, logical manner, you need to understand it, but creative thinking is born from instances where you don't understand something. The trick is probably in the mix. Let your child explore new information and form creative thoughts about it, then talk to him logically about it. Giving your child time to think freely about new information allows him to think about it in many contexts and many forms before being told which concept or form is proper.

In order to better develop your child's understanding of different concepts, her perception should be shaped by touching, hearing, and seeing something simultaneously, to experience the concept as best as she can. Take time to let your child talk about what she is seeing, touching, and hearing. By experiencing new concepts in different contexts, your child can become aware of different aspects of an idea and develop her understanding of its meaning.

Reasoning

There is more than one type of reasoning. Formal reasoning skills, such as deductive and inductive reasoning, are developed at a later age. The reasoning skill that is focused on in kindergarten is spatial-temporal reasoning, or the ability to visualize and transform objects in space.

Spatial-temporal operations are responsible for combining separate elements of an object into a single whole or for arranging objects in a specific spatial order. Spatial-temporal operations require successive steps; each step is dependent on previous ones.

Spatial-temporal skills are the most frequently tested reasoning/ thinking skills on IQ and other standardized tests. You can work on these skills with your child through the math and science activities in this book.

Logic

Children learn about and understand logical concepts in different ways. In math, for example, some kids think about numbers in terms of where they are on a number line; other kids think about how many objects make up each number. These children reach an understanding of numbers, their meaning, and how to use them, but they reach it in different ways. Taking this example further, these children comprehend the information and understand what numbers represent. But if one group is then asked to handle the numbers in different contexts, the group will need to be aware of different aspects of numbers in order to develop a fuller understanding of their meaning. The group can then think about numbers in different ways and apply them to different situations in a logical way rather than simply recall what they mean.

A large part of logical thinking stems from the ability to see objects and apply concepts in many contexts (spatial-temporal reasoning applies here). Teaching children to question information teaches them to think about the information in more than one context before making a logical conclusion about it. Logical thinking can be reinforced during the discipline process by applying a logical consequence to a behavior rather than an arbitrary punishment.

Kindergartners are still figuring out the properties of objects and are not yet able to reverse operations—that is, to understand that 250 ml of water in a tall, narrow glass and 250 ml of water in a large, flat pan are equal in volume. Their reasoning, from an adult perspective, is still illogical. Things that happen at the same time are thought to have a causal relationship to one other—for example, "Because I wore my new shoes, it rained."

Thinking Skills Activities

To help your child develop thinking skills, you can:

- Encourage her to ask questions about the world around her.

- Ask him to imagine what will happen next in the story when you are reading together.

- Actively listen to your child's conversation, responding seriously and nonjudgmentally to her questions.

- Ask what he is feeling and why when he expresses feelings.

- Suggest that she find facts to support her opinions and encourage her to locate information relevant to her opinions.

- Use entertainment—a book, a TV program, or a movie—as the basis of family discussions.

- Use daily activities as occasions for learning (environmental learning).

- Reward him for inquisitive and/or creative activity that is productive.

- Ask her what she learned at school.

Environmental Learning

There are thousands of ways that you can use your child's everyday environment to encourage thinking skills. Remember, if your child is an active participant in a home where there are "why" and "how" discussions, he or she is more likely to be an active thinker both in and out of school.

End of Kindergarten Thinking Skills Checklist

Students who are working at the standard level at the end of kindergarten:

___ Are moving toward abstract thinking

___ Are developing reasoning skills

___ Have difficulty making choices

Assessment

11

It may sound harsh, but your kindergartner will be assessed individually, and, if you are in a state that has learning and testing requirements, your child will also be assessed as part of a group. Assessment serves several different purposes:

1. Assessing individual student abilities and knowledge and adapting instruction accordingly

2. Evaluating and improving the instructional program in general

3. Determining individual student eligibility for promotion or graduation, college admission, or special honors

4. Measuring and comparing school, school district, statewide, and national performance for broad public accountability

There is more than one kind of assessment and more than one context in which this term is frequently used. There are multiple ways that you and your child's teacher assess your child. There is broad assessment of your child's knowledge of certain things and your child's performance as compared to other children of the same age and grade. Standardized assessment is usually done at the end of the year in later grades, and comprises many sessions of test taking in a short time period. There are uses for all types of assessment.

Assessing Individual Student Abilities and Knowledge

Students learn in different ways, so teachers assess their daily learning in different ways. The most common way to assess daily learning is by observing how your child responds to and implements things that he or she learns in the classroom. As teachers observe and consider the variety of daily assignments of students, they begin to help their students demonstrate this learning on tests.

Observation and Portfolio Assessment

Your child's overall progress is assessed by considering her developmental stage and cognitive learning abilities with key concepts and key skills within the framework of her learning style. Teachers (and by now, you) do this by observing your child on a daily basis, gauging reaction and comprehension time when given new information, and asking frequent, informal questions. All the activities in this book include explanations for how to assess your child's performance, and the checklists at the beginning and end of each chapter can help you assess her progress in each skill. Teachers have begun to implement portfolio assessment more frequently. Teachers are giving your child the opportunity to demonstrate learning through a variety of activities, such as art projects, writing activities, oral answers, and daily participation to determine the true levels of comprehension and skill development with the variety of materials and skills in each learning unit. Although many people think portfolio assessment is one of the most accurate methods of determining learning, it has been criticized for its subjectivity. Teachers try really hard not to be subjective; contrary to what some people think, they aren't likely to retaliate for a mishap with a parent by lowering the child's grades. When a child succeeds, the teacher has also succeeded. Discounting the child's success because of personal feelings destroys the teacher's professional success.

Standardized Testing

Testing is a hot topic, and rightly so. We all remember standardized tests—spending days filling in little circles with a number 2 pencil.

The majority of teachers dislike standardized testing for a number of reasons. Sure, there is the issue of accountability. But the heart of the issue is not that teachers are afraid of being held to a standard to keep their job—it is that they disagree with being held to what many of them believe is a false standard. Think about how an auditory or physical learner will do on a test designed for visual learners. The tests aren't an accurate picture of what all learners can do.

In defense of test makers, they are doing their best to adjust their approaches within the limitations of state requirements, logistical requirements, and traditional business practices. But the system within which teachers, parents, students, and the test makers are trying to operate is definitely imperfect.

Other issues are centered around "teaching the test." Teachers are afraid that the curriculum they are told to teach will be so narrowly geared toward the test that it will limit their ability to teach the things that support the tested items. They are concerned that they will be able to teach only to the cognitive learning level when they know that the student should also be able to apply the knowledge, synthesize it, and evaluate it. We have discussed how individual scores can be invalid, but so can group scores. Test results may be invalidated by teaching so narrowly to the objectives of a particular test that scores are raised without actually improving the broader, often more important, set of academic skills that the test should be measuring.

At the end of the day, assessment is a very strong tool. It encourages, discourages, and measures learning. Assessment should be a means of fostering growth toward high expectations and should support student learning. When assessments are used in thoughtful and meaningful ways and combined with information from other sources, students' scores provide important information that can lead to decisions that promote student learning and equality of opportunity. The misuse of tests for high-stakes purposes (tests that are used to make significant educational decisions about children, teachers, schools, or school districts) has undermined the benefits these tests can foster.

The standardized tests that cause so much controversy are norm-referenced tests, meaning that the test questions are selected so that a national sample of students' test scores will result in a normal distribution: there will always be a group of students at the bottom, a majority in the middle, and a group at the top. It is unrealistic to expect whole groups of students to be in the top percentiles (or groups) on these tests. Most students are expected to perform near the fiftieth percentile.

Helping Your Child Test Well

You play a vital role in helping your child succeed on standardized tests. Here are just a few of the things you can do:

- Put your child at ease by discussing your own experiences with taking tests. If you were nervous or anxious, talk about it. Let him or her know that those feelings are normal.

- Be aware of the specific days tests will be given. Ask your child how the testing sessions are going. Offer encouragement.

- Stress the importance of listening to test directions and following them carefully. Provide practice activities at home, such as following a recipe or reading and answering questions about a story.

- Make sure your child goes to bed early every night and at the same time every night, especially on the night before testing.

- Encourage healthy eating, rest, and exercise.

- Most standardized testing is given over a three- or four-day period. Ask your child's teacher for a schedule and make sure your child attends school on those days.

- Meet with your child's teachers to discuss the results. If your child had difficulty in specific areas, ask teachers for suggestions in the form of homework assignments, techniques, and specific material.

What the Scores Really Mean

High-stakes tests are used to make significant educational decisions about children, teachers, schools, or school districts. To use a single objective test in the determination of such things as graduation, course credit, grade placement, promotion to the next grade, or placement in special groups is a serious misuse of tests. Remember, your child's score on a standardized test is only one measure of what he or she knows. Most schools use multiple measures, including student projects, homework, portfolios, chapter tests, and oral reports.

Measuring and Comparing School, School District, Statewide, and National Performance for Broad Public Accountability

Increasingly, policy makers at the federal, state, and local levels want to identify ways to measure student performance in order to see how well the public education system is doing its job. The goals of this accountability approach include providing information about the status of the educational system, motivating desired change, measuring program effectiveness, and creating systems for rewarding and sanctioning educators based on the performance of their students.

The use of testing (in later grades) to change classroom instruction is central to the theory of standards-based reform. It assumes that educators and the public can agree on what should be taught; that a set of clear standards can be developed, which in turn drive curriculum and instruction; and that tests can measure how well students perform based on those standards.

Kindergarten Society 12

Kindergarten is unlike any other year in school for your child. Your child is developing socially and emotionally at a rapid pace. At the beginning of the year, some children may be shy and appear to lack initiative; other children may be too assertive. It is a time of testing and exploring social relationships. As children become comfortable with their teachers and peers, they usually gain more confidence, which helps them establish friendships and become an active part of the class.

Kindergartners are more emotionally stable than preschoolers. They are developing a sense of humor characterized by nonsense and playing with language. They may develop specific fears, such as being afraid of the dark. Kindergarten students take criticism, name-calling, and teasing very seriously because they still accept what is said at face value.

Tommy, Can You Hear Me?

Kindergartners love to talk, usually much more than they like to listen. Your child's intellectual development is reflected in the rapid growth of vocabulary and the power to express ideas. He or she is developing visual and auditory memory along with the ability to listen to others. Kindergartners can pick up another language and accurately imitate other people's intonations and inflections, but still need help distinguishing sounds.

Have you noticed how much your child likes to use a new word that she has learned? Rhyming, inventing new words, and using big words to "get her way," to win arguments, and to joke are new skills for your child and are popular activities for kindergartners. Your child will be given many opportunities to talk about what she is doing, what she sees, and what she hears to help her construct meaning and learn from her experiences. The language and ideas shared by others enable children to gradually organize and attach meaning to their daily observations and activities.

Kindergarten children have a powerful urge to discover new things and to figure things out. They ask lots of questions, and they love to play guessing games and solve riddles. Their curiosity leads them to figure out concepts and relationships and become interested in symbols. They enjoy listening to stories, but they do not learn much from paying passive attention to you or a teacher. Your child's intellectual growth comes from exploration, testing, and investigating rather than listening.

Teacher's Helper

No matter how hard it is for you to get your child to help at home, school is a different story. Do you remember that sense of pride you felt when your teacher selected you to deliver a note to the office? What about looking forward to your turn to pass out supplies to the class? Simple things like that haven't changed for the generations of students following you, including your own child. Kindergarten children are eager to be trusted with responsibility. They appreciate going on errands, helping grown-ups, bringing things from home, and suggesting solutions to simple problems. Though kindergartners are still in an egocentric phase, they can be very helpful and kind to each other when working in groups.

Capitalize on your child's willingness to help his teacher by asking him to do similar "jobs" for you at home.

Let's Get Physical

Does your child feel more tired when standing still than when running laps around the backyard? Yes, this is normal. Most kindergartners are full of energy and are ready to run, swing, climb, and jump, to test their strength. Does your little learner have rhythm? Kindergartners enjoy such activities as marching, jumping, or clapping to music, and they do a lot of that at school.

During kindergarten your child's physical growth has slowed down, and she is trying to get some control over her sensory development. Hand-eye coordination is still developing, along with fine motor skills. It is easy to load kindergartners up with activities that develop fine motor control—cutting, pasting, coloring, and writing. As important as these skills are, however, it is not in your child's best interest to concentrate on them all the time. Failing to mix fine motor skill development with activities that allow for growth of physical coordination will hamper your child's progress in both areas.

Here Today, Gone Tomorrow

Kindergarten is an important social milestone. Your child has entered into "kid society" by spending a large part of his day with lots of other children. For many, this is usually the first time students have been around many other children their own age at once. Your child may develop many friendships quickly because of his proximity to other kids. His feelings can oscillate greatly; one day he will think someone is the greatest friend, the next day not like him at all. You are going to be hearing "He's not my friend anymore." Don't take it too seriously. Kindergartners tend to be fickle and change their minds as frequently as their toys. Friendship is a relatively new experience and is being learned through watching others and mimicking them.

Up to now your child has been learning the basics of friendship (sharing, taking turns, playing together), but few of these skills have been practiced on the scale she will need when she starts school. Your child is seeing established friendships in older kids and sees kindergartners entering into friendships. Every day she is learning about social patterns and experimenting with friendships.

Adding to the mix is that your child is at an age when his general interests change a lot. If your child was wildly interested in soccer and is now into karate, he may feel that he doesn't have anything in common with his former friends and will seek new ones. Things are pretty black and white for five- and six-year-olds. If they think they have nothing in common with a friend, it is hard to get them to see other things they may share.

Kindergartners can easily have at least one person in particular whom they don't like at all and dread seeing during the day. It is not uncommon for bullying to start in kindergarten, so you should listen closely to determine if your child is consistently afraid of or dreads seeing a particular child. If she is experiencing these feelings, speak to the teacher to see if there is a problem with that child in school. Tell the teacher about your child's anxiety and work with him or her to come up with a solution to the problem.

Moving On to First Grade

13

Y ou made it! Your kindergartner is now going to be a first grader! You can monitor your child's readiness for first grade and determine areas that you can help your child reinforce with the following subject area and developmental checklists.

Ready to Go

Students who are ready to go on to first grade:

Reading

____ Know words have meanings

____ Know letters make words

____ Know all or part of the alphabet

____ Know most of the sounds each letter makes

____ Recognize familiar written words, such as their name

____ Recognize written words found in their daily environment

Writing

___ Form letters

___ Correspond sounds with writing

___ Name and label objects

___ Maintain focus

___ Gather, collect, and share information

___ Incorporate storybook language (for example, "Once upon a time") into their writing

___ Write in chronological order

Math

___ Understand that numbers are symbols that tell you how many

___ Know about time and can tell time to the nearest hour

___ Recite numbers one through twenty corresponding to flash cards

___ Combine and separate sets using objects

___ Classify and sort sets

___ Solve addition facts through 10

___ Compare more, less, and same

___ Recognize half of a whole object

Science

___ Investigate and experiment with objects

___ Observe, describe, sort, and classify objects

___ Participate in simple experiments to discover information

___ Communicate questions, make predictions, and make observations orally and/or in drawings

___ Describe and sort objects using the five senses

___ Compare the properties of objects, such as objects that float versus objects that sink

____ Identify how objects and animals move—slide, turn, twirl, or roll

____ Identify whether something is living or nonliving

____ Understand needs that plants and animals have in order to grow and the changes these organisms experience

____ Recognize properties of common earth materials, such as soil, water, and rocks

____ Observe and describe the daily weather and the four seasons

____ Describe ways to conserve natural resources

Social Studies

____ Understand why we have rules

____ Know about their school and the people there to help them learn

____ Can identify community helpers

____ Can explain what jobs certain community helpers do

____ Know how to find things in their own neighborhood

____ Know how to use a map

____ Can identify different holidays throughout the year

____ Can discuss the ways people celebrate holidays

Thinking Skills

____ Are moving toward abstract thinking

____ Are developing reasoning skills

____ Have difficulty making choices

Anxieties

There are always going to be anxieties when moving on to another grade. After all, you just got to know the kindergarten teacher, and you really, really like her. Who will be the homeroom mom next year? Wait—this is supposed to be about the children's anxieties, right?

Wrong. Everyone is going to feel a little sad, a little anxious, a little excited, and really glad it's summer when the subject of first grade first arises.

If your child's teacher has recommended that he or she be held back for a year, don't spend an excessive amount of time worrying about that. Kindergarten and first grade are the most appropriate times to hold a child back. Developmental growth is the most disparate at this age and is most easily corrected or brought up to grade level by reteaching the kindergarten building blocks as your child's cognitive and developmental growth enables him or her to fully grasp them. The absolute worst thing you can do is fight this.

The way you handle your child's repeating a grade will factor into his or her self-esteem for a lifetime. Do not be embarrassed, do not be ashamed, and do not assume your child is "slow." Your child needs extra time to develop skills that come with growth. Give him or her that time and the self-esteem that he or she deserves.

Minimizing "Brain Drain"

Now that your child has acquired tangible skills that are building blocks for future learning, you are facing your first year of the challenge of keeping those skills fresh. Here are some things to keep in mind to help your child retain his or her kindergarten skills during the summer months.

Do

- Reinforce skills from his or her kindergarten year through environmental learning.
- Go to the library on a regular basis.
- Include learning activities in your weekly summer routine.
- Encourage free and creative thinking through art projects or active play.

DON'T

- Try to "get ahead" for the next year.

- Have your child spend the whole summer with a tutor.

- Ignore obvious learning opportunities (such as mapping out the trip to Grandma's).

Your child's kindergarten year has been enhanced, supported, and furthered by your efforts. Over the summer and into first grade, continue creating the learning environment that you worked so hard on this year. You're on the right track—stay there or be square!

LITERATURE FOR KINDERGARTNERS

This section contains a list of books that your child may find interesting. There are also learning activities along with the reading selections. You can find more recommended literature for your kindergartner at www.knowledgeessentials.com.

Alexander and the Terrible, Horrible, No Good, Very Bad Day
Author: Judith Viorst
Publisher: Simon & Schuster

This book is about a little boy named Alexander and a day when nothing seems to go right. It starts early one morning when he wakes up with gum in his hair.

Special Considerations: Parents will have to read this book to their child, but the child should be able to read with the parent when they come to the title phrase.

Learning: Have your child compare this story to his own life. Ask your child if he ever had a day like Alexander. Let him describe his "bad" day.

Activity: Write a story about a bad day with a good ending.

Follow Up: Give your child a large sheet of white paper. Draw a line down the center. Ask your child to tell you about a very good day. Write what your child says on one side of the paper. Ask your child to tell you about a very bad day. Write what your child tells you about the bad day on the other side of the paper. Discuss the two days.

Blueberries for Sal
Author: Robert McCloskey
Publisher: Viking

The story takes place in Maine. A mother and her daughter go out to pick blueberries and so do a bear and her cub. Both the daughter and the cub stray to the other side of the hill and end up with the wrong mother. This is an excellent book for reinforcing the skill of comparing and contrasting.

Special Considerations: If your child hasn't experienced growing fruits, you might have to explain how the fruit grows. Buy some blueberries to share with your child after reading the book.

Learning: Your child can learn to compare two objects or things. You can also use this book to learn about words that start with the letter "B."

Activity: To help your child learn to compare and contrast, you can discuss what the people and the bears are doing that is alike and different. You can also discuss fruits and vegetables and how they are alike and different.

Follow Up: You can also use this book to teach your child about the letter "B." Make some blueberries out of paper and then have your child draw a picture that starts with "B" on each blueberry. Give her paper to make her own basket for her paper blueberries. To finish the project, paste the blueberries in the basket.

Chicken Soup with Rice

Author: Maurice Sendak
Publisher: Harper Trophy

This is a collection of cute poems written and illustrated by Maurice Sendak. Each poem begins with the name of a month and something that you can do with chicken soup with rice. This is an excellent book for beginning readers because of the poems' repetition and simple words, or for anyone else who would like to be reminded of his or her carefree childhood.

Special Considerations: Read this book to your child and then let him say the "chicken soup with rice" parts.

Learning: Your child will be able to learn the names of the months as well as what things are associated with each particular month.

Activity: Give your child his own pages titled with the names of the months and allow him to illustrate each one. You may need to talk about what happens in the months with your child.

Follow Up: Have your child illustrate his own ideas for each month. Have him include his own idea for what is special about each month.

Corduroy

Author: Don Freeman
Publisher: Viking

Corduroy is a story that children love because it's about that faithful childhood friend, the teddy bear. Corduroy is a teddy bear in a department store waiting for someone to take him home. One day a little girl sees him and wants to buy him, but her mom says he doesn't look new because he's lost the button on one of the shoulder straps of his green corduroy overalls. That night when the shoppers are gone, the bear goes searching for his lost button and has quite an adventure!

Special Considerations: You and your child will need to read this book together.

Learning: You can discuss fact and fiction with your child. Could this story really happen?

Activity: It's always intriguing to imagine what toys and other inanimate objects might do when we're not around. *Corduroy* is a good story to use during a theme unit on imagination. After reading the book, show the Disney video *Toy Story,* another imaginative tale of toys that come to life, or *The Brave Little Toaster,* a story of household appliances that go in search of their master. Have your child use her imagination and tell you what she thinks her toys do when humans aren't around.

Follow Up: Of course, *Corduroy* can also be used to do research to learn about the real thing. You'll find lots of information at the Web site www.bearden.org. As interesting facts are discovered, have your child write them on bear-shaped paper and display them on the refrigerator, or take a day and go with your child to the zoo to see real bears.

Green Eggs and Ham
Author: Dr. Seuss
Publisher: Random House

Everyone knows the tale of Sam-I-Am trying to convince his friend to eat green eggs and ham! The rhymes are repeated through the book, with new ones added on. "I would not, could not with a fox, I would not, could not in a box . . ." This is a great book for rhyming words!

Special Considerations: Although you will first have to read this book with your child, he will quickly pick up on the rhyming.

Learning: This is an excellent book to discuss rhyming words, such as "Sam" and "am."

Activity: After reading the book, review the rhyming words. Have your child brainstorm more pairs of rhyming words with you. Using story paper, help him write his own pairs of rhymes. For example: "A ghost ate some toast." Next have him draw pictures to go along with the rhymes.

Follow Up: Make your own green eggs and ham! Have your child help make scrambled eggs with green food coloring. You can soak ham in water and food coloring the night before to achieve a green look. Now you can have a colorful snack while you read the book again.

The Snowy Day
Author: Ezra Jack Keats
Publisher: Viking

Peter is excited about the snowfall. He bundles up and enjoys playing in the snow. Peter makes a snowman and angels in the snow, and pretends to be a mountain climber. Later he goes inside, enjoys a steamy bath, and then looks for the snowballs he brought inside. As he goes to bed, he remembers the pleasures of "a snowy day."

Special Considerations: If you live in a climate where it never snows, you might have to help your child understand what snow is and what activities you can do in the snow.

Learning: Have your child guess what Peter finds in the snow that makes a special track. Before you read the story, have your child make predictions of what she thinks Peter might do as he spends a day outside in the snow.

Activity: Have a snowball fight with your child. Make snow angels with your child. Make footprints in the snow. Make a snowman. If you don't live in a climate with snow, you can adapt the activities. Have a snowball fight with wads of paper. Make angels and footprints in sand instead of snow. Make a snowman out of Styrofoam balls.

Follow Up: In the story, Peter makes a little snowball and places it in his pocket. Later he discovers that the snowball is no longer there. Ask your child what she thinks happened to the snowball. Do an experiment by having your child make a snowball, place it in a container, and then predict what will happen.

There's a Nightmare in My Closet

Author: Mercer Mayer
Publisher: Puffin Books

A little boy has a scary monster in his closet. When he finds the courage to shoot the monster, he discovers that the monster is just as scared as he is.

Special Considerations: You will have to read this book to your child.

Learning: This is a good story to use for teaching the words "in" and "out."

Activity: Have your child draw a large picture of his closet. On separate sheets of paper, have him draw things he is afraid of and cut them out and put them in the drawing of the closet. Things he is not afraid of he puts out of the closet.

Follow Up: Ask your child if he has ever been afraid to go to sleep. What could you do to help make it easier for your child to go to sleep?

Tikki Tikki Tembo

Author: Arlene Mosel
Publisher: Henry Holt

In this folktale from China, we learn that mothers used to give their eldest sons very long names. One day Tikki Tikki Tembo falls into a well, and Chang, his younger brother, runs home to tell his mother what happened. Chang is out of breath and very excited, so it takes him a long time to tell his mother what happened. Tikki Tikki Tembo is eventually saved, but we learn why all Chinese children now have shorter names.

Special Considerations: You will need to read this book to your child.

Learning: This book could be used for comparing and ordering numbers.

Activity: Give your child a strip of paper. Have her write her full name on the piece of paper and then count the number of letters in the name. Write the number of letters in her name on the back of the piece of paper. Then, on another piece of paper, write out Tikki Tikki Tembo's full name. Compare the length of the names by counting the letters.

Follow Up: Have your child write other people's full names and then count the number of letters and write it on the back of the piece of paper. Have your child arrange the names from greatest to smallest and then smallest to greatest.

The Velveteen Rabbit
Author: Margery Williams
Publisher: Doubleday

A boy receives a stuffed bunny for Christmas, and it is put inside the toy closet with the other things he received. There the bunny is teased by the mechanical toys, who claim they are real because they move. A worn skin horse reassures the bunny that no toy can become real until it is wholeheartedly loved by a child. Eventually the boy finds the rabbit, plays with it, and shares the joys of his childhood with it. One day the boy becomes really sick, and the doctor explains to the boy's parents that the child is seriously ill and to throw away the ragged rabbit, for it may now be a carrier of the disease. The sick child cries out for his stuffed rabbit and is brokenhearted to learn that he will never have it again. Thanks to fairy magic, the rabbit becomes real and eventually visits the child, now grown, to see what has become of his beloved friend.

Special Considerations: You will need to read this book with your child.

Learning: Your child can learn about what is real and not real.

Activity: Have your child get out all of his stuffed animals. Which ones represent something real?

Follow Up: Take your child to a pet store or veterinarian and ask the owners about the different types of rabbits and how to care for one.

Where the Wild Things Are
Author: Maurice Sendak
Publisher: HarperCollins

Where the Wild Things Are is the classic tale of young Max, who is sent to bed without supper. Max dreams that he is in the land of the wild things and is king. But Max misses his home, so he sails back. He finds dinner waiting for him!

Special Considerations: You will have to read this book to your child.

Learning: Use this book to give descriptions of the characters.

Activity: Have your child choose a "wild thing" character from the book and describe it for you. If she is giving you only physical characteristics, then ask questions to get her to tell you how the character acts or is feeling.

Follow Up: Talk about characters in other books—any book that contains a favorite character of your child.

SOFTWARE FOR
KINDERGARTNERS

Are you eager to use your computer as a learning tool? I bet you told yourself that educational software is the real reason you needed to get that upgraded media package. Here is the chance to redeem yourself. This appendix provides a list of software titles that are appropriate and interesting for kindergarten learners. You can find more recommended computer resources for your kindergartner at www. knowlegeessentials.com.

The Playroom
Broderbund

This software introduces letters, numbers, and time concepts. Through interactive learning activities, children will gain knowledge of addition and subtraction, counting to twelve, and telling time to the nearest hour on both a clock face and a digital clock. Children will also recognize capital and lowercase letters, associate letters with words, and acquire spelling and keyboarding skills.

Product Focus: Kindergarten basic skills sets

Candy Land Adventure
Hasbro Interactive

This software develops such skills as letter sequencing, counting, memory, and matching. In addition, children apply decision-making skills, build confidence, and enhance their imaginations. The software includes matching games, mazes, and other age-appropriate activities.

Product Focus: Kindergarten basic skills sets

Zurk's Learning Safari
Soleil

This software lets children explore natural science, reading, and math. There are six different puzzles that will also help your child with shape recognition, decision making, following directions, and observation skills. The software encourages children to learn early reading and math skills through the enjoyment of animal puzzles.

Product Focus: Kindergarten basic skills sets and science concepts

JumpStart Kindergarten
Knowledge Adventure

This product focuses on pre-reading, early math, language, and creative arts. The software contains a "learning profiler" that helps in determining your child's learning style and adjusts the play and pace to accommodate your child. There is a motivating reward system to keep children interested, and all the games are based on state education standards.

Product Focus: Kindergarten basic skills sets

Trudy's Time and Place House
Edmark

Your child will build time-telling skills and explore the concept of time by controlling an animated movie. Trudy, the main character, also teaches geography, helping children develop mapping and direction skills. They will also "travel" the world and learn about the continents, oceans, and major landmarks.

Product Focus: Kindergarten time concepts, basic directions, and map skills

Thinkin' Things Collection 1
Edmark

This software focuses on memory development, logic, visual and spatial thinking, music memory, and problem solving. There are question-and-answer and explore-and-discover sections that give your child an opportunity for structured and independent learning. The software can automatically adjust to your child's individual learning level.

Product Focus: Observation and memory skills, problem solving, and creativity

WiggleWorks
Scholastic

This product provides instruction in the key areas of reading, writing, and language. The software allows children to read, write, speak, and record themselves reading. They can also change the activity books, print them, and share them with others. The interactive software emphasizes multiple forms of print concepts, encouraging children to become more confident and fluent readers.

Product Focus: Kindergarten language skills

Millie's Math House

Edmark

Children explore fundamental math concepts as they learn about numbers, shapes, sizes, quantities, patterns, sequencing, addition, and subtraction. Some of the fun activities include counting critters, building mouse houses, creating crazy-looking bugs, and finding just the right shoes for Little, Middle, and Big.

Product Focus: Kindergarten math skills

James Discovers Math

Broderbund

This software has songs, stories, and interactive activities to teach early math concepts that encourage problem solving, reasoning, and creativity. Based on the real-life experiences of an Australian boy, the program uses a broad selection of familiar objects to promote math learning. There are ten different math games that will help children learn and practice basic math skills.

Product Focus: Kindergarten math skills

Sammy's Science House

Edmark

This software helps build early science and thinking skills. Children sort names of plants, animals, and minerals at the Sorting Station. They also build toys and machines in the Workshop, learn about animal habitats at Acorn Pond, and manipulate weather variables with the Weather Machine. The program also gives positive feedback and rewards while guiding students toward success. There is a question-and-answer and explore-and-discover section that gives children an opportunity for structured and independent learning.

Product Focus: Kindergarten science skills

KINDERGARTEN
TOPICAL CALENDAR

This calendar tells you approximately when the skills covered in this book are presented during the school year. There will be variances, of course, but for the most part the skills build on one another, so it is logical that your child will learn things in a certain order.

Reading	Writing	Math	Science	Social Studies
September				
Knows all or part of the alphabet	Has control over hand movement and holds writing tool correctly	Recites numbers one to twenty corresponding to flash cards	Investigates and experiments with objects (observes, describes, sorts, and classifies)	Understands why we have rules
October				
Identifies letters	Is interested in writing and associates it with communicating wants and needs	Writes and recognizes numerals	Describes and sorts objects using the five senses	Learns about school and the people there to help her

Reading	Writing	Math	Science	Social Studies
November				
Knows words have meaning	Forms letters	Understands that numbers are symbols that tell you how many	Participates in simple experiments to discover information (communicates questions, makes predictions, and makes observations orally and/or in drawings)	Learns about families and different cultures
December				
Knows that letters make words	Corresponds sounds with writing	Recognizes shapes and recalls names of shapes	Compares the properties of objects, such as objects that float versus objects that sink	Identifies different holidays throughout the year and the way people celebrate these holidays
January				
Recognizes familiar words, such as names	Names and labels objects	Classifies and sorts sets	Identifies how objects move—slide, turn, twirl, or roll	Learns about communities and community helpers
February				
Recognizes written words in his environment	Maintains focus	Compares more, less, and same	Identifies living and nonliving and learns what living plants and animals need in order to grow and change	Learns about different types of communities
March				
Holds a book the correct way and turns pages front to back	Can gather, collect, and share information	Combines and separates sets using objects; solves addition facts through 10	Understands the properties of common earth materials, such as soil, water, and rocks	Learns that communities are made up of neighborhoods and what a neighborhood is

Reading	Writing	Math	Science	Social Studies
April				
Can retell favorite stories	Incorporates story-book language (i.e., "Once upon a time") into writing	Recognizes half of a whole object	Observes and describes the daily weather and the four seasons	Learns how to find things in her own neighborhood
May				
Knows most of the sounds each letter makes; can use the sounds to sound out the letters in a word, but may not be able to form the word	Can write in chrono-logical order	Knows about time and can tell hours	Describes ways to conserve natural resources	Learns how to use a map

GLOSSARY

accountability   Holding students responsible for what they learn and teachers responsible for what they teach.

achievement test   A test designed to efficiently measure the amount of knowledge and/or skill a person has acquired. This helps evaluate student learning in comparison with a standard or norm.

assessment   Measuring a student's learning.

authentic assessment   The concept of model, practice, and feedback in which students know what excellent performance is and are guided to practice an entire concept rather than bits and pieces in preparation for eventual understanding.

benchmark   A standard by which student performance can be measured in order to compare it and improve one's own skills or learning.

Bloom's taxonomy   A classification system for learning objectives that consists of six levels ranging from knowledge (which focuses on the reproduction of facts) to evaluation (which represents higher-level thinking).

competency test   A test intended to determine whether a student has met established minimum standards of skills and knowledge and is thus eligible for promotion, graduation, certification, or other official acknowledgment of achievement.

concept An abstract, general notion—a heading that characterizes a set of behaviors and beliefs.

content goals Statements that are like learning standards or learning objectives, but which describe only the topics to be studied, not the skills to be performed.

criterion-referenced test A test in which the results can be used to determine a student's progress toward mastery of a content area or designated objectives of an instructional program. Performance is compared to an expected level of mastery in a content area rather than to other students' scores.

curriculum The content and skills that are taught at each grade level.

curriculum alignment The connection of subjects across grade levels, cumulatively, to build comprehensive, increasingly complex instructional programs.

developmental delay A significant lag in meeting certain developmental indicators or growth milestones. A small lag is not considered to be a developmental delay. Developmental delay is often considered as the precursor to the label "disabled" for children from birth to nine years old.

developmental disorder One of many disorders that interrupt normal childhood development, such as autism, dyslexia, and Asperger syndrome. They may affect a single area of development (as in specific developmental disorders like dyslexia) or several (as in pervasive developmental disorders like autism). With early intervention, most specific developmental disorders can be accommodated and overcome.

high-stakes testing   Any testing program whose results have important consequences for students, teachers, colleges, and/or areas, such as promotion, certification, graduation, or denial/approval of services and opportunity.

IQ test   A psychometric test that scores the performance of certain intellectual tasks and can provide assessors with a measurement of general intelligence.

learning disabilities   Disorders that involve understanding or using written or spoken language. They cause substantial difficulties in listening, speaking, reading, writing, or math. Learning disabilities may occur with conditions such as emotional disturbances or sensory impairments, but are not necessarily caused by them.

learning objectives   A set of expectations that are needed to meet the learning standard.

learning standards   Broad statements that describe what content a student should know and what skills a student should be able to demonstrate in different subject areas.

measurement   Quantitative description of student learning and qualitative description of student attitude.

median   The point on a scale that divides a group into two equal subgroups. The median is not affected by low or high scores, as is the mean. (See also **norm**.)

metacognition   The knowledge of one's own thinking processes and strategies, and the ability to consciously reflect and act on the knowledge of cognition to modify those processes and strategies.

multiple-choice test   A test in which students are presented with a question or an incomplete sentence or idea. The students are expected to choose the correct or best answer or completion from a menu of alternatives.

norm   A distribution of scores obtained from a norm group. The norm is the midpoint (or median) of scores or performance of the students in that group. Fifty percent will score above the norm and 50 percent will score below it.

norm group   A random group of students selected by a test developer to take a test to provide a range of scores and establish the percentiles of performance for use in determining scoring standards.

norm-referenced test   A test in which a student or a group's performance is compared to that of a norm group. The results are relative to the performance of an external group and are designed to be compared with the norm group, resulting in a performance standard. These tests are often used to measure and compare students, schools, districts, and states on the basis of norm-established scales of achievement.

outcome   An operationally defined educational goal, usually a culminating activity, product, or performance that can be measured.

performance-based assessment   Direct observation and rating of student performance of an educational objective, often an ongoing observation over a period of time, and typically involving the creation of products dealing with real life. Performance-based assessments use performance criteria to determine the degree to which a student has met an achievement target. Important elements of performance-based assessment include clear goals or performance criteria clearly articulated and communicated to the learner.

performance goals   Statements that are like learning standards or learning objectives, but they describe only the skills to be performed, not the content to be studied.

portfolio assessment   A systematic and organized collection of a student's work that exhibits to others the direct evidence of the student's efforts, achievements, and progress over a period of time. The collection should involve the student in selection of its contents and should include information about the performance criteria, the rubric or criteria for judging merit, and evidence of student self-reflection or evaluation. It should include representative work, providing a documentation of the learner's performance and a basis for evaluation of the student's progress. Portfolios may include a variety of demonstrations of learning.

BIBLIOGRAPHY

Brainerd, C. J. (1978). *Piaget's Theory of Intelligence.* Upper Saddle River, N.J.: Prentice Hall.

Evans, R. (1973). *Jean Piaget: The Man and His Ideas.* New York: Dutton.

Lavatelli, C. S. (1973). *Piaget's Theory Applied to an Early Childhood Curriculum.* Boston: American Science and Engineering.

London, C. (1988). "A Piagetian Constructivist Perspective on Curriculum Development." *Reading Improvement, 27,* 82–95.

Piaget, J. "Development and Learning." In C. S. Lavatelli and F. Stendler (eds.), *Reading in Child Behavior and Development.* Orlando: Harcourt Brace, 1972.

———. (1972). *To Understand Is to Invent.* New York: Viking.

Shure, M. B. (1993). *Interpersonal Problem Solving and Prevention: A Comprehensive Report of Research and Training.* A five-year longitudinal study, kindergarten through grade 4, no. MH-40801. Washington, D.C.: National Institute of Mental Health.

Shure, M. B., and G. Spivack. (1980). "Interpersonal Problem Solving as a Mediator of Behavioral Adjustment in Preschool and Kindergarten Children." *Journal of Applied Developmental Psychology, 1,* 29–44.

———. (1982). "Interpersonal Problem-Solving in Young Children: A Cognitive Approach to Prevention." *American Journal of Community Psychology, 10,* 341–356.

Sigel, I., and R. Cocking. (1977). *Cognitive Development from Childhood to Adolescence: A Constructivist Perspective.* Austin, Tex.: Holt, Rinehart and Winston.

Singer, D., and T. Revenson. (1978). *A Piaget Primer: How a Child Thinks.* New York: International Universities Press.

Willis, M., and V. Hodson. (1999). *Discover Your Child's Learning Style.* New York: Crown.

INDEX